THE POETIC SCRIPTURES OF PAUL

THE POETIC SCRIPTURES OF PAUL

GOD'S WORD IN RHYTHM & RHYME

MICHAEL D. WESTER

LIGHTHOUSE PUBLICATION
SPREADING THE WORD OF GOD, ONE BOOK AT A TIME.

Printed in the United States of America
ISBN 978-1-64133-631-4 (sc)
ISBN 978-1-64133-632-1 (hc)
ISBN 978-1-64133-633-8 (e)

Library of Congress Control Number: 2019917229

Artwork and Cover Design by ***Cameron Klingenberg***

Inspirational / Worship and Devotion / Non-Fiction
19.11.15

Lighthouse Publication
1553 E. Caro Road
Caro, MI 48723

www.lighthousepublication.com

CONTENTS

INTRODUCTION

I leaned over to hug my dad as he lay in his bed. Tears flowed from his eyes and mine as we said our final goodbyes on this earth. He was dying. Yet in the final weeks of his life, he found comfort in studying God's Word. He would not just read, but he would take notes, recording them in a notebook. Even though he knew his death was imminent, he sought to discover and learn as he had done for most of his adult life. He lived his final day as if he was going to live another day. God's Word gave him that outlook. He did not wait to die. He lived each day until he died.

This third book of The Poetic Scriptures is dedicated to the memory of my dad. We loved discussing the many difficult passages found throughout the letters of Paul. This book encompasses all thirteen of those letters.

A team of several pastors and devoted students of God's Word served to check over this poetic translation to ensure its accuracy. Thank you to the following: Jason Garwood, Bill Livingston, David Roberts, Jon Terry, Tony Tomasino, Jeff Vogel, Doug Wallaker, Pat Wester, Bruce Winters, and Sam Woodard.

Two symbols are placed throughout the work to alert the reader: an asterisk (*) and a diamond (◆).

An asterisk (*) indicates that the word or phrase is a departure from the biblical text. For example, Romans 1:3 has an asterisk following the line, *Who is a human, indeed.* This means that Paul did not specifically state this. However, the phrase does fit in with the next lines which emphasize Jesus's humanity. This example is typical of this usage of poetic license.

A diamond (◆) indicates that the word or phrase is an expansion on the biblical meaning of a word or phrase. For example, Romans 2:3 has a diamond preceding the words, *and conclude*. Paul is addressing a person who judges. The action word *judge* is based upon a drawn conclusion. So I rendered the line *You who judge ◆and conclude*. Another example that illustrates this usage is 1 Corinthians 13:12. The last two lines read:

> But then we will see face to face
> When there arrives perfection.◆

The last line is a poetic elaboration on the word *then* in the first line. When is then? Paul gave that answer in verse 10, when the perfect comes.

This book was very challenging in many respects. Complicated sentence structures and lengthy sentences are typical for the apostle Paul. I simplified them by breaking them up into smaller sentences. For example, Ephesians 2:1-3 is one sentence in Paul's mind. Many translations break it up into two or more sentences. I did it in four. Lists of various sorts are given by Paul. In order to produce rhyme with the proper rhythm, some of them are not listed in the same order. These are just a few examples of the challenges I faced. The end result, however, still accurately reflects God's Word.

May this book help you to dive deeply into God's Word. And may it be implanted it in your heart and mind for His glory.

THE POETIC LETTER TO THE ROMANS

1:1 Paul, a bond slave of Christ Jesus,
Called to be an apostle
Who has been set apart by God
For the purpose of His gospel.

1:2 Long beforehand God had promised,
By means of the prophetic[1] voice
Written in the holy Scriptures,
This gospel about His choice.

This gospel is about His Son,
1:3 Who is a human, indeed,*
Since He was born of David's line,
Since He is of David's seed.

1:4 He also is the Son of God.
In power this was conveyed
When resurrecting from the dead,
From the tomb where He was laid.*

This also showed that His spirit
To holiness did accord,
Proving that He's not just the Christ,*
But He's Jesus Christ our Lord.

1:5 Through Him we have received this grace,
Apostleship as it's termed,
Sent out[2] to bring Gentiles to faith,
Among whom *yours is confirmed.

1:6 You are the called of Jesus Christ,
The fruit* of those who were sent
To serve for the sake of His name.
For you this letter is meant.*

1:7 To all of you who are loved by God,
Who live in the city of Rome,
Who are called to be set apart
To serve Him and Him alone.*

To all of you *I write these words:
Grace and peace on you are poured,[3]
Which proceed from God our Father
And from Jesus Christ the Lord.

1:8 I thank my God through Jesus Christ
For you all, first and foremost,
Because your faith is being spoken
Throughout the whole world, *almost.

1:9 God, whom I serve with my spirit
In the gospel of His Son,
Is my witness of my prayers,
Yes, each and every one.*

He knows how I remember you
Always, whenever I pray,
1:10 Constantly petitioning Him
That at last I'd come your way.

But I ask with one condition,
That in God's will I succeed.
1:11 Although* I long to see your face,
In His will, I must proceed.*

Why do I long to see your face?
In order that I can share
A spiritual gift of some kind
That strengthens you *when I'm there.

1:12 That is to say in other words,
That in you will intertwine
Encouragement through the faith
Of each other, yours and mine.

1:13 I do not want for you, brothers,
To be uninformed of my tries,
That often times I planned to come,
But prevention did arise.

It's been this way to the present,
As I've served in all the miles,*
So that among you I'll have fruit
As the rest of the Gentiles.

1:14 For I am in obligation
To both the wise and the fools,
To both Greeks and barbarians,
And that obligation rules.*

1:15 So then, I am very eager,
Yes, eagerness is my tone,*
To preach the gospel, the good news,
To you all who are in Rome.

1:16 For unashamed is what I am
Of the gospel. This is why:
It is the power of God to save
All who in Him, faith apply.[4]

The gospel first came to the Jews,
And then to the Greeks it came.
The gospel is God's power to save◆
All who believe in Christ's name.◆

1:17 For in the gospel is revealed
That righteousness God does give
Only by faith, as is written,
"The righteous by faith will live."[5]

1:18 For from heaven the wrath of God
Has been revealed against sin,
Against mankind's ungodliness
And unrighteousness within.

The ungodly and unrighteous,
In sin the truth they restrain
1:19 Because that which is known of God
Within them is very plain.

1:20 For since the world was created,
His unseen nature is eyed
Through the product that He has made,
Being understood deep inside.

They can see His eternal power.
His divineness they can deduce
Through the product that He has made.
So, they are without excuse.

1:21 For even though they knew of God,
They did not praise Him as such.
"Worthless" described their reasoning,
And their heart was darkened much.

1:22 Even though they claimed to be wise,
To fools they were rearranged.
1:23 The glory of God immortal
For an image they exchanged.

They exchanged the immortal God
For images with these features:
Mortal man, and four-footed beasts,
And birds, and crawling creatures.

1:24 So, God gave them up in their lusts,
Embedded within their hearts,
To the vileness of debasing
Among men their body parts.

1:25 God gave them up for exchanging
The truth of God for the lie.
They served and worshipped creation.
God, they did not glorify.

They served and worshipped creation
And not Him who created.
He is to be praised forever.
This is the truth[6] *now stated.

1:26 Because of this, God gave them up
To passions that just degrade.
Many examples I will cite*
So that my point can be made.*

Females decided to exchange
The nature of their design
For that which is against nature.
To disgrace they did resign.*

1:27 Likewise the males, abandoning
The nature of the female,
Burned with passion for each other.
Their lust they did not curtail.*

Men among men performed vile acts,
Among themselves receiving
The necessary penalty
For the error of their cleaving.

1:28 Just as humans deemed it worthless
To have God in them entwined,[7]
God gave them up to their thinking,
To a vile and worthless mind.

1:29 This resulted in wrong lifestyles,
Being filled with sins of all brands,
Unrighteousness and wickedness,
Covetous and evil hands.

Full of envy, murder, and strife,
Deceit, and malevolence;
Gossips, slanderers, haters of God,
Also, those full of violence.

1:30 There's the arrogant and boastful,
Authors of wrong and ill-worth,
Those who rebel against parents
From whom they had their birth.*

1:31 There's the foolish and the faithless,
Those who lack mercy and love.
These are the many examples*
That bring judgment from above.*

1:32 Now the righteous sentence of God
All of these have known within,
That those who practice such lifestyles
Deserve to die in their sin.

And in the face of this verdict
They not only in sin persist,
But they give their full approval
To such lifestyles *in this list.

2:1 Therefore, O man, you've no excuse,
All of you who judgment pass.
In that which you judge another,
Condemnation you amass.

For you yourself do the same things,
2:2 And this we know to be true:
God's just judgment is upon all
Who practice such things like you.

2:3 Or do you have this reasoning,
You who judge ◆and conclude
But still practice the same things,
That God's judgment you'll elude?

2:4 Or what about God's character?*
With kindness He overflows.
His forbearance and endurance
Are for what, do you suppose?

Do you despise His character,
Of this fact being ignorant,
That His kindness tends to lead you
Not to sin, but◆ to repent?

2:5 But according to your own heart
That is unchanged and hardened,
You're storing up wrath for yourself,
And you will not be pardoned.*

The day of wrath, it will arrive,
Coming with revelation
Of the righteous judgment of God
Upon all of creation.*

2:6 He will render what's due to all
According to what's been done,
Whether that work is good or bad.*
Yes, God will reward each one.◆

2:7 God will render eternal life
To those who keep seeking these:
Honor, glory, eternity,
While patient in good deeds.

2:8 But to those who live by self-will
And who in wrong deeds engage,
Who are unfaithful to the truth,
God will reward wrath and rage.

2:9 Tribulation and great distress
On all those who evil seek,
Each and every soul of man,
To the Jew first, then the Greek.

2:10 But glory and honor and peace
To all those who good works seek,
Each and every soul of man,*
To the Jew first, then the Greek.

2:11 So, before God, there exists not
Any partiality,
For He does not play favorites◆
With any ethnicity.◆

2:12 For all who do not have a law[8]
And have sinned without that guide,
They will perish without a law.
They cannot be justified.*

Likewise, all who do have a law
And have sinned against that guide,
They'll be condemned by that law.
They cannot be justified.*

2:13 For not the hearers of a law
Before God are declared right.
Only the doers of a law
Are justified in His sight.

2:14 For when Gentiles who have no rules
Naturally practice the Law,
Although they have no outside guide,
In themselves a guide they draw.

2:15 For they show the works of the Law
As written in their hearts,
While their conscience is their witness,
And a judgment, it imparts.

So, their reasoning becomes their law,
And them that law may accuse,
Or their reasoning defends them,
And so, that law may excuse.

2:16 In that day God will judge men's hearts,
And there's nothing they can hide.
This judgment is through Jesus Christ,
And by my gospel, it's applied.

2:17 Now let's suppose you are a Jew,
Or at least that is your claim,[9]
You lean on law and boast in God,
2:18 And His will, you ascertain.

You discern what is important,
For by the Law you are taught,
And so you have convinced yourself
With these credentials you've got.*

2:19 You think that you are qualified
To be a guide to the blind
And a light to those in darkness,
A teacher to every kind.*

2:20 For since you have within the Law
The form of knowledge and truth,
You think yourself as the teacher
Of spiritual◆ fools and youth.

2:21 Therefore, you who teach another,
To yourself, do you apply?
You who proclaim, "You must not steal,"
Your stealing, do you deny?

2:22 "Do not commit adultery,"
To another you convey.
Do you commit adultery?
Do you apply what you say?◆

You who express your abhorrence
Of idols that have been made,
Do you rob the pagan temples
And then profit from that raid?[10]

2:23 You who boast in legalism,
Are you dishonoring God
By your transgression of the Law
So yours would not be outlawed?[11]

2:24 It is written ◆in prophecy,
"Blasphemy Gentiles commit,
Speaking evil against God's name,
Because you're a hypocrite."[12]

2:25 Circumcision benefits you
If you practice law, nonetheless,
But it becomes uncircumcision
If against law you transgress.

2:26 Therefore, if one uncircumcised
Keeps the Law's righteous demands,
What of his uncircumcision?
Circumcised by God[13] he stands.

2:27 And he who is uncircumcised,
In the flesh, *I mean to say,
Will judge you as a lawbreaker
At the time of judgment day.*

Although you have these two things:
Circumcision and the Law,
You will be judged by those who have
Not one of these at all.

2:28 In defining who is the Jew
Or of being circumcised,
What is outward or physical
Must never be emphasized:*

2:29 A true Jew is one inwardly,
Circumcised inside the heart.
It's not about the written Law
But one's spiritual part.

A true Jew is not one who seeks
Praises from the public eye,
But a true Jew is one who seeks
His praises from God *on high.

3:1 In light of this, what advantage
Belongs to the Jew by birth?
And what about circumcision?
What is its value and worth?

3:2 Advantages and worth abound
Unto the Jewish nation.
Primarily, God entrusted
To them His revelation.

3:3 So, what if some were unfaithful,
Would their failure render void
The faithfulness of the Lord God?
Would His word then be destroyed?*

3:4 There is no way this can happen,
For even though man is found
To be faithless* and a liar,
To truthfulness God is bound.

The purpose of His faithfulness
Has been written with detail:
"So that Your words be proven right,
And when judged, You will prevail."

3:5 So, if our own unrighteousness
Brings the righteousness of God out,
Is God unjust in showing wrath?
(Human thinking is what I spout)

3:6 There is no way this can be true,
For how will God judge mankind?
We can come up with more ideas*
Of a faulty human mind.*

3:7 For example,* if in my lie
God's truth for His glory swells,
Why then am I still being judged
As a sinner who rebels?

3:8 Why not say (as some say we teach,
But us, they falsely indict),
"Let us do wrong so good will come."?
His condemnation is right!

3:9 Therefore, are we better? No!
We've proved it's no opinion
That all people, Jew and Gentile,
Are under sin's dominion.

3:10 As is written in the Scripture,
"No one is righteous, not one.
3:11 There's no person who understands.
No person seeks God; there's none.

3:12 "From right◆ all have deviated.
Jointly useless, they became.
No one practices what is good.
Not one *can make that claim.

3:13 "Their throat is like an opened tomb,
The air, the stench of death grips.*
With their tongues they keep deceiving,
Snake venom under their lips.

3:14 "Cursing, bitterness fills their mouth.
3:15 Their feet are swift to shed blood.
3:16 Crushing ruin and misery
All throughout their pathways flood.

3:17 "The path of peace they did not know,
They did not come to realize.◆
3:18 The respect and the fear of God
Has no place before their eyes."

3:19 Now we know that what the Law says
Speaks to all those within its sphere,
So every mouth may be silenced,
And the world, God's judgment may hear.

3:20 For this reason, no flesh will be
Declared righteous in God's eyes
By means of works contained in law,
For sin through law we realize.

3:21 The righteousness that God does give
Has been shown apart from law.
It is not gained by works, just faith,[14]
As the written Word foresaw.*

The Law and the Prophets witnessed
3:22 That the righteousness one receives
Comes through faith in Jesus the Christ,
To everyone who believes.

For distinction does not exist
3:23 Because sin is each one's story.
Everyone fails to measure up
To the standard of God's glory.

3:24 All believers are called righteous
As a free gift by God's grace
Through the redeeming act of Christ
When Jesus died in our place.*

3:25 God put Jesus on full display,
And His wrath was satisfied.[15]
He paid sin's debt* in His shed blood,
And by faith ◆it is applied.

This sacrifice demonstrated
His righteousness there and then,
For He put up with all past sins,
Passing over the sins of men.

3:26 So, God punished sin in Jesus
To declare Himself as just,
While also declaring righteous
He who in Jesus has trust.

3:27 So, where is there room for boasting?
It is eliminated.
Not through a law of works, but faith,
All boasting is negated.

3:28 For we conclude that a person
Becomes righteous in one way,
Apart from works contained in law,
Through a law of faith, we say.

3:29 Does God belong to Jews only?
Does He not to Gentiles too?
God belongs to Jews and Gentiles,
Yes, ◆this is certainly true.

3:30 For God is one God *over all,
And righteousness He'll allot
To the one whose faith ◆is in Christ
Whether circumcised or not.

3:31 Therefore, do we by means of faith
Render all law nullified?
Not at all! For by faith ◆in Christ
Law's fulfillment is supplied.

4:1 So then, what shall we say about
Our forefather Abraham,
The father of the Hebrew race?
What had been found by this man?

4:2 Let us assume that Abraham
By his works was justified.
He would have boasted before God,
But we read* of no such pride.

4:3 For what does the Scripture declare?
"In God, Abraham believed.
Faith was counted as righteousness."
So, righteousness he received.◆

4:4 So, in regards to one who works,
His wages do not accrue
In accordance to a free gift
But according to what is due.

4:5 As for the one who does not work,
But in God, he truly relies,
His faith is deemed as righteousness.
The sinner, God justifies.

4:6 Likewise, David pronounces
This blessing upon the man
To whom God credits righteousness
Apart from works, *understand:

4:7 "How blessed are those whose lawless deeds
Are forgiven ⬩and wiped clean.
How blessed are those whose sinful deeds
Have been covered ⬩and not seen.

4:8 "How blessed is the man against whom
The Lord will never count sin."
4:9 So, tell me then of this blessing,*
It is on what kind of men?*

Only him who's circumcised,
Or the uncircumcised man?
Remember* faith was counted as
Righteousness for Abraham.

4:10 At what time was he given this,
While in a circumcised state,
Or while he was uncircumcised?
Of this there is no debate.*

He was given this righteousness
Not in a circumcised state
But while he was uncircumcised.
Of this there is no debate.*

4:11 For Abraham received from God
Before the fleshly removal
The symbol of circumcision
As a seal ◆of God's approval.

The seal is righteousness by faith
So Abraham could become
The father of those who believe,
Yes, all of them, ◆not just some.

Righteousness is credited to
Those who are uncircumcised.
He's their father, if they have faith.
As a son they're recognized.*

4:12 He's father of one circumcised,
Not just physically defined,[16]
But spiritually◆ he's father of
The Jew whose faith is this kind:*

A faith which follows in the steps
Of our father Abraham
Who had faith while uncircumcised.
So as righteous, he did stand.*

4:13 For the promise ◆that God had made
To Abraham and his seed
That he would inherit the world
Came only one way indeed.*

The promise did not come through law,
But it came through just one way,*
Through righteousness that is by faith.
Of this there is much to say.*

4:14 If they are heirs who lean on law,
Then faith has been negated,
And the promise •that God has made
Has been annihilated.

4:15 You see, the Law produces wrath
Since through law sin does persist,*
But where there is no law at all,
Transgression does not exist.

4:16 Because of this, it is by faith
So by grace it would accord,
So that heirship be dependent
On a promise •by the Lord.

The promise is to all his seed,
Not just those who follow law,
But those too from Abraham's faith.
He's the father of us all.

4:17 This is confirmed by the Scripture
In one more of my citations,*
"I, the Lord have appointed you
The father of many nations."

He then believed before the Lord
Who brings to life what is dead
And calls things which do not exist
As if they exist instead.

4:18 He believed God against all hope
In the face of the absurd.•
Yet his belief was based on hope
In the promise of God's word.•

"Your descendants will be like this,"
Came one of God's confirmations.*
He believed God so he'd become
The father of many nations.

4:19 Now Abraham had considered
His body as good as dead,
For he had lived one hundred years,
But he believed God instead.*

Abraham had considered too
Sarah's womb as void of life,
But he believed that God would give
The promised seed through his wife.[17]

4:20 In unbelief, he wavered not
Toward the promise that God swore,
And since he gave God the glory,
His faith was empowered more.

His faith was made even stronger
4:21 Since he was fully assured
That the Lord God was capable
To fulfill His promised word.

4:22 Therefore, it says, "It was counted
To him as righteousness."
4:23 This word applies not just to him,
4:24 But to us it does address.

For us it too will be counted
As righteousness, *as was said,
For us who believe in the One
Who raised our Lord from the dead.

4:25 The Lord Jesus was given up
For our sin's condemnation.
He was then raised up from the dead
For our justification.

5:1 Therefore, we have peace before God
Through Jesus Christ our Lord
Since by faith we've been justified.
Righteousness He did record.*

5:2 By faith we have through Jesus Christ
Gained access into this grace,
The free gift◆ in which we now stand.
Pride in God's glory we place.

5:3 Now not just this, but we take pride
In our afflictions as well
Because we know that they produce
Patience ◆within us to dwell.

5:4 In turn, that patience produces
A character that's approved.
That character, then produces
A hope *that cannot be moved.

5:5 This hope is not a simple wish*
But one that disappoints not
Because it's based upon God's love
Which to us in Christ, He brought.*

God's love has been poured out to us,
(All self-gain it did expel),[18]
Poured in our hearts through His Spirit
Given us ◆to indwell.

5:6 For while we yet were without help
And to weakness did resign,*
Christ died in place of the godless,
And it was at the right time.

5:7 For rarely will one die in place
Of one who's righteous ◆and just.
Perhaps someone will die in place
Of one who's good, *full of trust.

5:8 In stark contrast, God demonstrates
His own love toward us *in grace,
For even though we were sinners,
Christ gave His life in our place.

5:9 Now, since we've been declared righteous
In the blood of Christ, ◆God's Son,
How much more will we all be saved
Through Him from the wrath to come.

5:10 If God made peace by His Son's death
While as rebels we behaved,
How much more, being reconciled,
Will we by His life be saved.

5:11 Now we also take pride in God
Through Jesus Christ our Lord,
Through whom we now have received peace.
With God, we're in one accord.[19]

5:12 Sin entered the world by one man.
By means of that sin came death.
Because everyone also sinned,
From them too was swiped their breath.

5:13 Sin was already in the world
Before law was the regime,
But sin is not charged without law,
And yet death still reigned supreme.

5:14 Death reigned from Adam to Moses,
(Yes, death no one could forbid),*
Even over those who sinned not
In the same way Adam did.

Now Adam himself typifies
The One who was yet to come,
5:15 But his sin does not equate with
The gift *of the Coming One.

For if by means of one man's sin,
The many were made to die,
How much more did the grace God gives
To the many multiply.

Grace was given through the one Man,
The one Man, Jesus the Christ.
This grace is free; ◆it's undeserved;
Its value cannot be priced.*

5:16 What came through Adam and the gift,
There is no correlation.
Judgment came out of just one sin
Effecting condemnation.

But the free gift came out of sins,
Not one, but many, *it's true,
Effecting the declaration
Of righteousness *through and through.

5:17 If by means of the sin of one
Through that same one death did reign,
Much more will those who receive grace
Through Christ in life do the same.

The grace received is abundant.
Righteousness, the gift is termed.
It comes through the One, Jesus Christ.
Through Jesus it is affirmed.*

5:18 Therefore, just as through the one sin
Condemnation on all did fall,
So also through that one right act
Righteousness of life comes to all.

5:19 Just as through one man's rebellion,
"Sinners" the many were named,
So too through the One's compliance,
"Righteous" they will be proclaimed.

5:20 Now when law came alongside sin,
Then sin multiplied galore,
But wherever sin multiplied,
Grace multiplied all the more.

5:21 As sin reigned in death, so also
Through righteousness, grace would reign,
Which results in eternal life
Through our Lord Jesus Christ. *What gain!

6:1 In light of this, what will we say,
"Then let us in sin persist
In order to receive more grace."?
6:2 No, may that never exist!

How is it even possible
For us who to sin have died
To persist in living in sin?
We cannot in sin abide.[20]

6:3 Or else do you ignore the fact
That those baptized into Christ
Were baptized too into His death,
His life for sin sacrificed?*

6:4 Through our baptism into death
We were all buried with Him
So that as Christ was raised from death,
A new life too we'd begin.

As Christ was raised from death by this,
The Father's omnipotence,
So we also are empowered
In the new life to commence.

6:5 For if we have been joined with Him
In the likeness of His dying,
Surely in His rise from the dead
We should live as that's implying.

6:6 Why? Because we know that with Him
Our old self was crucified
To make useless the sinful self
So in sin we'd not abide.

6:7 For the one who has truly died,
From sin he has been set free
That no longer as a servant
To the sin master he would be.[21]

6:8 If we truly have died with Christ,
We'll live with Him, we believe,
6:9 Because we know that Christ was raised
From death forever to leave.

Death no longer rules over Him,
6:10 For the death that He had died
Had everything to do with sin.
For all time it was applied.

The life He lives, He lives to God.
6:11 So, in life and death *then strive.
Reckon yourselves as dead to sin,
But to God, in Christ[22] alive.

6:12 Therefore then, stop allowing sin
In your mortal body to reign,
For this results in obedience
To its lusts ◆that are profane.

6:13 Stop presenting your body parts
As weapons for sin to use
As a means of unrighteousness.
This life is no life to choose.*

Present yourselves ever to God
As being alive from the dead,
And your body, all parts, to God
As righteous weapons instead.

6:14 For sin will not rule over you.
It's mastery has no place*
Because you are not under law.
Instead, you are under grace.

6:15 Therefore, should we on occasion
Commit a sin here and there[23]
Since we're not under law but grace?
To conclude this do not dare.[24]

6:16 Don't you know that when you present
Yourselves as slaves to obey,
That you are slaves to whatever
You keep letting have its way?

Either sin ◆can be your master,
Resulting in death, no less,
Or it can be obedience,
Resulting in righteousness.

6:17 But praise to God because of this,
That though to sin you were slaves,
You, from the heart, came to obey
The gospel teaching *which saves.

You were given to that teaching,
6:18 And so from sin, you were saved,*
And having been set free from sin,
To right you became enslaved.

6:19 (Now I use this analogy,
Of slavery, I mean to say,◆
Because of your fleshly weakness,
Of your struggle to obey)◆

You presented your body parts
To unclean and lawless deeds,
Which resulted in lawlessness.
As slaves you yielded to these.

As you did that, so do this now:
As slaves give your body parts
To righteousness, which results in
Holy and sanctified *hearts.

6:20 For when you were enslaved to sin,
From righteousness you were free,
6:21 And in those things that shame you now
What kind of fruit did you see?

The end of all those things is death.
There was no fruit anyhow.*
6:22 But since you have been freed from sin,
You possess your fruit right now.

Set free from sin, enslaved to God,
Your fruit leads to holy deeds,
And what's the end of that journey?
To eternal life, it leads.

6:23 For death is sin's compensation,
But God gives a gift that's free.
It's in our Lord, Jesus the Christ.
It's life for eternity.

7:1 Or are you, brothers, ignorant
(To you who know law, I say)
That only while one is alive,
The Law over him holds sway?

7:2 For a married woman is bound
To her man while his life remains,
But when he dies she stands released
From the law which to him pertains.

7:3 Therefore, if while her husband lives
She joins with another man,
She would be called, "Adulteress!"
This joining the law does ban.*

If her husband happens to die,
From the marriage law, she's free.
So, when she marries another,
An adulteress she wouldn't be.

7:4 You, my brothers, in like fashion
To the Law came to be dead
By means of the body of Christ
So to Him, you would be wed.

I am speaking of Jesus Christ*
Who was raised up from the dead.
So that for God we would bear fruit
Is why to Christ we were wed.*

7:5 For while we were yet in the flesh,
Sinful lusts by the Law revealed
Were working in our body parts
That for death the fruit would yield.

7:6 But from the Law we've now been freed
Since death we have undergone,
Dying to that which held us down,
To sin, to which we were drawn.*

This death results in our service,
A life of service. *Hear it!
In oldness of the letter? No!
In newness of the Spirit.

7:7 Therefore, what should we then conclude,
That the Law is sin? No way!
For I would not have realized my sin
Without a law *to obey.

For example, take coveting,
I would not have known at all,
But the Law said, "Do not covet,"
7:8 And to that sin I did fall.

And sin then took advantage of
The commandment to embed
In me all kinds of coveting,
For without law sin is dead.

7:9 Now I myself once was living
Without any law applied,
But then when the commandment came,
Sin revived, and then I died.

7:10 The commandment, which was designed
To result in life instilled,
It did result in death for me
7:11 Because sin deceived and killed.

The commandment became for sin
An opportunistic tool.
It took advantage of the Law
Both to bring death and to fool.

7:12 So then, the Law, it is holy
And the commandment as well.
It is holy, righteous, and good.
In all ways it does excel.*

7:13 In light of this, should we conclude
That that which was good to me
Imparted death *instead of life?
No! May it never be!

But sin came to be shown as sin
By that which is good ♦and grand.
Sin killed me by means of the Law,
Sin exposed by the command.

The commandment showed me the truth
That sin did truly abound.
Through the command sin was sinful,
Very sinful it was found.

7:14 We know the Law is spiritual,
But having to sin been sold,
I myself was only fleshly.[25]
In bondage, my sin did hold.[26]

7:15 For I was not even aware
Of that which I produced,
For what I did not wish to do
By that sin, I was seduced.

For that very thing I hated,
In it, my practice just stood.
7:16 Since I practiced what I wished not,
I agreed that the Law is good.

7:17 So then, it was no longer me
That produced what I knew not,
But it was sin indwelling me
Since I did not as I ought.*

7:18 So then, I knew that within me,
In my flesh, I mean to state,
7:19 No good indwelled, for though willing,
No good could I cultivate.

7:20 If I practiced what I wished not,
Then what I produced unknown[27]
Was no more done by me but sin
Which in me had made its home.

7:21 Therefore, although I wished to do
That which is good, *and not sin,
I found this law at work inside,
That evil is there within.

7:22 For with the Law given by God
I did joyfully agree
Deep within the inner being,
7:23 But another I did see.

Another law I saw in me,
That is the bodily part,
Warring with God's Law in my mind
And captivating *my heart.

That law is called the law of sin
Which in my body did dwell,
Warring with God's Law in my mind,
Capturing *my heart as well.

7:24 And then I cried,◆ "O what a man,
A miserable man I am!
Who will save me from this body,
This body of death? Who can?"

7:25 Thank God through our Lord Jesus Christ.
From this He made me afresh:*
Serving God's Law within my mind
But sin's law within my flesh.

8:1 Therefore, in this present era
In which Christ Jesus has come,*
There exists no condemnation
For those who are in God's Son.[28]

8:2 For the law used by the Spirit,
Which is life in Jesus Christ,
Has freed you from sin and death's law
Through what Jesus sacrificed.*

8:3 For what the Law could never do,
Weakened by the flesh of men,
God accomplished in His own Son
For the purpose to condemn.

He sent His Son in the likeness
Of the sinful flesh of mankind.
Concerning sin, God in Christ's flesh,
Condemnation He assigned.

8:4 This was so the Law's requirement
Would within us be achieved
Who do not live after the flesh
But the Spirit *whom we've received.

8:5 For those who live after the flesh,
On these things they concentrate:
The matters that are of the flesh,
The sinful flesh that's innate.◆

Those who after the Spirit live,
On these things they concentrate:
The things that are of the Spirit,
His things, I articulate.*

8:6 The thinking of the flesh brings death,
But from this there is release,*
For the thinking of the Spirit
Brings life and also peace.

8:7 As for the thinking of the flesh,
It's hostile toward God, *you know.
Unto God's Law it won't submit.
It cannot even do so.

8:8 Those in the flesh cannot please God,
For the flesh only rebels.*
8:9 You're in the Spirit not the flesh
If in you the Spirit dwells.

If anyone does not possess
The Spirit of Christ ◆the King,
That one does not belong to Him.
To Jesus he cannot cling.*

8:10 Although mortal is the body
Due to the effects of sin,
Our spirit is alive by this:
The righteousness *that's in Him.

That's assuming Christ is in you,
8:11 That the Spirit lives inside,
And so if that is really true,
This promise can be applied:*

The Spirit of Him who raised Christ,
Raised Him from death's avenue,
Will revive your mortal bodies
Through His Spirit who's in you.

8:12 Therefore, brothers, as to the flesh
We are not debtors at all
To live according to the flesh,
For a lifestyle is its call.[29]

8:13 For if you live after the flesh,
If in the flesh you exist,
You are surely destined to die
If you in that life persist.

However, if by the Spirit
You keep on putting to death
The sinful deeds of the body,
You'll surely live *and have breath.

8:14 For all those who have the Spirit
As their leader and their guide,
These are truly the sons of God
8:15 Who've gained the Spirit inside.

For you have not gained a Spirit
Of slavery again to fear
But a Spirit of adoption,
In whom you cry, "Father dear."

8:16 The Spirit, He with our spirit,
In testimony unflawed,*
Jointly gives the attestation
That we are children of God.

8:17 Now if we are children of God,
Then also we are His heirs,
And each of us along with Christ
In His inheritance shares.

That's assuming that we suffer
With Jesus *(who was abhorred)
So that we will be glorified
Together with Him, *our Lord.

8:18 Now as for the present sufferings,
They're unworthy, is my call,
To be compared to the glory
That will be shown to us all.

8:19 For creation's eager longing
Awaits with expectation
The showing of the sons of God,
This future revelation.

8:20 The creation was subjected
To a vain and aimless state,
Not by its choice, *but by the curse
Of the One who did create.[30]

The subjection was based on hope
8:21 That creation's future state
Will be freedom from corruption.
So, in slavery it does wait.

The freedom from its corruption
Is a freedom of the kind
That belongs to all God's children,
Or glory, as it's defined.

8:22 For we know that the creation,
That is, each and every piece,
Has been groaning and suffering pains
Up to now *without decrease.

8:23 Not only them, but we ourselves
Are just filled with groans and cries
While we await our adoption
When our body, back He buys.

We continue to groan and cry,
Although we possess inside
The first fruits which is the Spirit
Who within us does abide.*

8:24 Now in this hope we all were saved,
But if we hope by our sight,
This is no hope because who hopes
For that which is seen outright?

8:25 If we keep on placing our hope
In the things we cannot see,
Through much patience we will await,
And we'll await eagerly.

8:26 Likewise, there's help from the Spirit
While in weakness we endure,
For we don't know what we should pray
Or how we should pray for sure.[31]

But while we groan in wordless ways,
While in our ignorant state,*
The Spirit brings our groans *to God.[32]
For us, He does mediate.

8:27 And the One who searches the hearts
Knows what is the Spirit's mind,
Namely, for saints He mediates,
But by God's will He's confined.

8:28 Yet we do know that all things work
Together for good, *no doubt,
For the good of those who love God,
Those by His purpose called out.

8:29 For those whom God resolved to know[33]
He predestined to this end:
To be conformed to the image
Of His Son *whom He did send.

This was for the very purpose
That Jesus as firstborn be
Over brothers of great numbers,
Having the authority.[34]

8:30 And those whom God did predestine
He also called ◆to believe,
And those He called, He justified,
And glory those will receive.[35]

8:31 Therefore, what then will we conclude
About these things we've disclosed?
Since it's true that God is for us,
Then to us who is opposed?

8:32 God who did not spare His own Son
But gave Him up in our place,
How will He not freely give us
All things with Christ *in His grace?

8:33 Who will produce a charge against
Those elected by God's hand?
He is the one who justifies.
So then, righteous they do stand.*

8:34 Who is the person that condemns?
The Christ is the one who died,
Even better, He was raised up
And now sits on God's right side.

Who is the person that condemns?
The Christ has earned that right*
Who mediates on our behalf,
And He does this day and night.[36]

8:35 Who will sever us from Christ's love?
Will pressure or stress outpoured,
Persecution or nakedness,
Famine, peril, or sword?

8:36 Just as it says in the Scripture,
"For Your sake *it is this way:
We were deemed as sheep for slaughter,
Being killed the entire day."

8:37 But in all these adversities
Are we victors? Oh, much more!
Not in ourselves but through the One
Who loved us *long before.

8:38 For I am convinced that from us
8:39 Nothing at all can sever
God's love in Jesus Christ our Lord,
Nothing at all, not ever!◆

Not death or life, angels or kings,
Not things now or yet to come,
Not powers, height, or even depth,
Or other creatures, not one!

9:1 I am speaking the truth in Christ,
My conscience testifying
With me in the Holy Spirit,
That in this I'm not lying:

9:2 Constant sorrow is in my heart.
My grief is very weighted,
9:3 For I myself could almost wish[37]
That I be separated.

Separated from Jesus Christ
In all of my brothers' place,
Brothers after the flesh, I mean,
Kinsmen of the Jewish race.

9:4 I'm referring to Israelites,
To whom belong and who saw
The adoption and God's glory,
The covenants and the Law.

And the service in the temple,
All the promises *now penned,
9:5 The lineage from the Patriarchs,
From whom Christ did descend.

Now that descent is from the flesh,
But what more will we say then?*
He's over all. He's also God.
He's blessed forever. Amen!

9:6 It's not as though God's word has failed,
For not all who have descent
From the lineage of Israel
Are Israel ◆as is meant.

9:7 Nor are they all children because
Abraham's bloodline they've claimed,
For this was said to Abraham,
"In Isaac, your seed will be named."

9:8 In other words, children by flesh
Are not God's children indeed,
But the children of the promise,
Yes, they are counted as seed.

9:9 This word is a word of promise,
"At this time next year, I'll come,"
(God was speaking to Abraham)*
"By Sarah will be a son."

9:10 Not just to her, to Rebecca
A promise was made.◆ Now hark.*
She conceived by only one man,
Being Isaac our Patriarch.

9:11 Although the twins were not yet born
Nor right nor wrong had they tried,
God gave these words so His purpose
Of election would abide.

9:12 This election is not by works
But by Him who gives the call.
"The older will serve the younger,"
Was told to her, *and that's all.

9:13 As we can see this was fulfilled,*
For in Scripture it is stated,
"Jacob I have chosen to love,
But Esau I have hated."

9:14 In light of this, what will we say?
God is not unjust, is He?
There's only one answer to give:*
No way! May this never be!

9:15 For to Moses God did make plain,
"I'll have mercy on whom I choose.
And I will shower compassion
On whom I want it to ooze."[38]

9:16 So then, mercy is not derived
From a person's wish or will,
Or a person's running pursuit,
But God who has mercy still.

9:17 For the Scripture says to Pharaoh,
"I raised you *to royal worth
To show My might in you and spread
My name into all the earth."

9:18 In light of this, we must conclude
There are no qualifiers.*
He has mercy and He hardens,
Depending on His desires.

9:19 Therefore, will you then say to me,
"Why does He still blame a man?
For who's able to make a stance
Against His determined plan?"

9:20 Whom do you think you are, O man,
To talk back to God, I say?
The molded won't ask the molder,
"Why have you made me this way?"

9:21 Does not the potter have the right
From one lump of clay to make
One vessel for dishonored use,
The other for honor's sake?

9:22 What if God, though wishing to show
His wrath and make known His strength,
Took vessels of wrath made for ruin
And endured them at great length?

9:23 What if He did this◆ to make known
His glorious riches *as planned
In vessels of mercy which He made
For glory long beforehand?

9:24 What if He did all this◆ for us
Whom He called *with great patience,
Not only from among the Jews
But also Gentile nations?

9:25 Just as He says in Hosea,
I quote words of the Divine,*
"The ones who are not My people,
I'll call them people of Mine."

Now He, the Lord, does not stop here*
But continues to decree,*
"I will call them My beloved,
The ones now unloved by Me.

9:26 "And in the place where it was said,
'You are not people of Mine,'
There they'll be called the sons of God,
The living God, ◆the Divine."

9:27 Isaiah cries out for Israel,
"Although its number be raved
As the sand that's on the seashore,
The remnant will just be saved.

9:28 "The Lord Himself will execute
On the earth this word decreed,
Accomplishing it completely
And decisively with speed."

9:29 Even as Isaiah predicts,
"If God[39] had not left us a seed,
We would have become as Sodom
Or like Gomorrah, *yes indeed."

9:30 So, of Gentiles what will we say?
That righteousness they obtained
Even though they pursued it not,
That righteous by faith they're named.

9:31 Of Israel, what will we say?
That though they kept in pursuit
After a law of righteousness,
For law's goal, they bore no fruit.

9:32 For what reason *did they fall short?
Because by faith it was not,
But as by works *they chased the goal,
And they stumbled *as they sought.

They tripped over the stumbling stone,
9:33 As written *in Isaiah's book,
"I am laying in Zion this:
A stone and a rock. Now, look!

"A stone that trips, a rock that riles
(He will be the Anointed),*
All who rest their faith upon Him
Will not be disappointed."

10:1 My petition for them, brothers,
Which before my God ◆is waved,
And the pleasure of my own heart
Is that my kinsmen be saved.

10:2 For I bear them testimony
That for God they have a zeal
But not according to knowledge,
A personal one that's real.[40]

10:3 For they ignore God's righteousness,
Seeking to gain their own kind.
The righteousness that God does give,
To it they have not resigned.

10:4 You see, Christ is the end of law,
Which only He could achieve,*
Resulting in a righteousness
Given to all who believe.

10:5 For Moses writes of righteousness,
Based on what law was to give,
"The man who does the things of law,
In those statutes he will live."

10:6 But righteousness which comes by faith
Puts it the following way,
As pertaining to faith in Christ,*
What we should or should not say:*

"Within your heart don't ever say,
'Into heaven who'll ascend?'"
(That is to say, to bring Christ down,
For Him from there God did send).*

10:7 "Nor say, 'Who will descend to hell[41]
After breathing their last breath?'"*
(That is to say, to bring Christ up,
For from there He raised* from death.)

10:8 But it says what? "The word is near,
In your mouth and in your heart."
That's the message we're proclaiming,
One of faith. *So hear this part:

10:9 If you confess with your own mouth
Jesus as Lord and believe
In your heart that God raised Him from death,
Salvation you will receive.

10:10 For in your heart it is believed
For a righteous declaration,
And in your mouth it is confessed,
Resulting in salvation.

10:11 For it declares in the Scripture,
Regarding the Anointed,*
"All who rest their faith upon Him
Will not be disappointed."

10:12 For there exists no distinction
Between the Greek and the Jew,
For the same Lord is over all
And not over just a few.*

For He is rich to everyone
Whose outcry to Him relates,
10:13 For "All who call on the Lord's name
Will be saved." •as Scripture states.

10:14 Therefore, how is it possible
For them upon Him to call
When they have not believed in Him?
That's not possible at all!*

And how then is it possible
To believe when they've not heard?
And how can they possibly hear
Without one who proclaims •the word?

10:15 And how can the unsent proclaim?
Just as Scripture does record,
"How lovely are the feet of those
Who bring good news *from the Lord."

10:16 But not all gave obedience
To the news that they had heard,
For Isaiah speaks about this,
"Lord, who has believed our word?"

10:17 Therefore, in light of what's been said,
This fact cannot be ignored:*
That faith comes by hearing the word,
The word about Christ •the Lord.

10:18 But did they fail to hear, I ask?
No! The opposite is true:
"Their voice went out into the earth,
All the earth •through and through.

"And also all their messages,
Yes, all of their orations,◆
Permeated all the borders
Of all their habitations."

10:19 Did Israel fail to know, I ask?
No! ◆These Scriptures I will quote.
First listen to what Moses says.
Then Isaiah's boldness, note.[42]

"By that which is not a nation,
You to envy I'll provoke.
By a nation, a foolish one,
I'll make you in anger smoke."

10:20 "By those who were not seeking Me,
I was found and discovered.
To those who asked not about Me,
I was shown and uncovered."

10:21 He also says to Israel,
"Throughout the entire day,
I've stretched My hand to a people
Who rebel and disobey."

11:1 In light of this, I am asking,
God has not then put away
His very own people, has He?
This we should never say!

For I myself was also born
As an Israelite indeed,
Belonging to Benjamin's tribe.
I am from Abraham's seed.

11:2 God has not cast out His people,
Those whom He resolved to know.[43]
Do you recall Elijah's case,
How before God he did go?

The Scripture states he pleads to God
Against Israel *(he's annoyed),
11:3 "Lord, they have killed your own prophets,
And Your altars they've destroyed.

"I myself am the only one
That remains *faithful to You,
And now my life they are seeking."
11:4 But what's the divine review?

The Lord answered, saying to him,◆
"Seven thousand, each a male,
I've reserved and left for Myself
Who've not bowed the knee to Baal."

11:5 Therefore, also, in the same way,
Currently *it's the same case.
A remnant has come to exist
According to choice by grace.

11:6 Because it is by means of grace,
By works it can never be
Since the meaning of the word grace
Would have to then change, *you see.

11:7 Therefore, what truth can we now state?
That which Israel pursues,
They obtained not, save the chosen.
The rest became hardened ◆Jews.

11:8 "A dazed spirit God gave to them,"
Even as the Scriptures say,
"Eyes that don't see, ears that don't hear,
Even to this very day."

11:9 And David says, "Let their table
To them become as a snare,
As a net, and as an offense,
And as a payback to share.

11:10 "And let their eyes become darkened,
So dark that they cannot see,
And let their back *be burdened much
And bent continuously."

11:11 Therefore, I ask, did Israel
Stumble to such a degree,
Resulting in their final fall?
No! May this never be!

But because of their transgression,
To Gentiles salvation came
To provoke them to jealousy
So salvation they would gain.*

11:12 Assuming that their transgression
Brings riches to the world scene
And their loss, riches to Gentiles,
Much more will their fullness mean.

11:13 I am speaking to you Gentiles,
And I hold in high esteem
My ministry to the Gentiles,
As an apostle, *I mean.

In this service, I hope that I
11:14 Might provoke my countrymen,
My Jewish flesh to jealousy
That I might save some of them.

11:15 For if the world is reconciled
Because of their rejection,
Then what will their acceptance bring? -
Except the resurrection!

11:16 Now if the first fruit is holy,
The whole harvest is. *It's true.
Also if the root is holy,
The branches are holy too.

11:17 Now let's assume that some branches
Were broken off, *which we see,
And you as a wild olive branch
Were grafted into the tree.

And you became a partaker
In the olive tree's rich root,
11:18 Then stop your boasting against these,
The branches *that bore no fruit.

But if you continue to boast,
Recall that this truth remains:*
You yourself don't support the root,
But it's you the root sustains.

11:19 In response to this you will say,
"Branches were cut off, *you see,
For the purpose that I myself
Be grafted into the tree."

11:20 Fine! Yes, by their unfaithfulness
They were broken off. That's clear.
Yet you yourself stand firm by faith.
So stop your boasting, but fear.

11:21 For if God spared not the branches
That by nature did abide,
Neither will He do that to you
If you remain in your pride.*

11:22 So then, observe God's character,
He is both kind and severe.
On those who fell, severity,
To you, God's kindness came near.

That's assuming in His kindness
You continue to remain,
Or otherwise, yes, you yourself
Will be cut off just the same.

11:23 But assuming their faithlessness
They no longer pursue,
They'll be grafted back in again,
Which God is able to do.

11:24 For let's assume that you yourself
Were from a tree cut away,
An olive tree that naturally
Grew in the wild, let's say.

If in a tree, an olive tree,
That's nurtured, *I underscore,
You were grafted against nature,
Then this is true all the more:

Those who are the natural branches,
Although cut off, as we see,*
Most certainly will be grafted
Into their own olive tree.

11:25 Brothers, about this mystery
I don't want you unaware
In order that within yourselves
Wisdom you'll not declare.

For a hardening only in part
In Israel has been paved
Until the Gentile harvest is done.
11:26 Thus all Israel will be saved.

As it is written, "From Zion,
The Rescuer will arise.
Ungodliness from Jacob
He'll remove *before My eyes.

11:27 "And this will be My covenant,
That within the heart begins,*
That I Myself will make with them
When I take away their sins."

11:28 In relation to the gospel,
The Israelites, they are foes,
Which is for your sakes, *Gentiles,
To which the gospel now goes.*

In relation to election
As beloved, they remain
For the sake of the Patriarchs
Through whom the promises came.*

11:29 Let me explain *a little more
Before from this I move on.*
The gifts of God and His calling
Can never be withdrawn.

11:30 For you were unfaithful to God,
The time before *you believed,
But due to their unfaithfulness
God's mercy you've now received.

11:31 Likewise they've now been unfaithful
In the mercy given you
With the result that *at some time
They'll receive mercy too.

11:32 For in their disobedience,
All men God has confined
For the purpose that He might give
Mercy to all mankind.

11:33 The wealth, the wisdom, and knowledge,
Which God has, O how vast!
His judgments are unsearchable,
His ways are unsurpassed.

11:34 For who's really known the Lord's mind?
Who's been His counseling aid?
11:35 Who first gave anything to Him
And by Him must be repaid?

11:36 By Him, through Him, also for Him,
Exist all creation, then;
To Him alone is the glory
For eternity. Amen!

12:1 Therefore, brothers, by God's mercies
I'm giving you this advice:
Present your bodies before God
As a living sacrifice.

Both holy and pleasing to God
Must characterize it too,
For that is your priestly service,
Which is logical to do.

12:2 And to this world stop conforming,
But keep on being transformed
By the renewal of your mind
So that this will be performed:*

That you will test and will approve
The qualities of God's will,
That which is good, and well-pleasing,
And perfect *to fulfill.

12:3 For through the grace given to me
As an apostle,[44] I speak
To each one who is among you,
Whether you be Jew or Greek.*

About yourself don't think higher,
Loftier than what you ought,
But think soundly according to
The faith God did allot.

12:4 You see, multiple body parts
Just one body does contain,
But each one of those body parts
Do not operate the same.

12:5 Likewise in Christ, though we're many,
We are one body, *brothers,
And each of us are body parts
Belonging to the others.

12:6 Because we have gifts that differ
In accordance with God's grace
Which was to us distributed,
To work them we must embrace.*

Whether that gift be prophecy,
Employ that gift as you ought[45]
According to the proportion
Of the faith, God did allot.

12:7 And whether that gift be service,
In your serving do the same;
Or whether that gift be teaching,
In the teaching, •you explain.

12:8 If that gift be encouragement,
Encourage as you ought
According to the proportion*
Of that faith God did allot.*

If that gift be one of giving,
Be generous in your grace.
If that gift be one of leading,
With diligence interlace.

If that gift be showing mercy,
In cheerfulness as you ought
According to the proportion*
Of that faith God did allot.*

12:9 In whatever gift you employ,[46]
Let your love be as it should,
Without any hypocrisy.
Hate the bad; grip the good.

12:10 In reference to brotherly love,
Work hard to like each brother.
In reference to showing honor,
Give preference to one another.

12:11 In reference to your diligence,
Hesitancies don't afford.
In reference to your attitude,
Be fervent; serve the Lord!

12:12 In reference to your hope ◆in Christ,
Continuously rejoice.
In reference to tribulation,
Let endurance be your choice.

In reference to your petitions,
Be both persistent and true.[47]
12:13 Contribute to the needs of saints.
Hospitality pursue.

12:14 Speak well to your persecutors.
Keep blessing and never scorn.
12:15 Rejoice with those who jump for joy.
Even weep with those who mourn.

12:16 Toward one another think the same.
Yourselves do not elevate.
Stop becoming a know-it-all.
With the humble associate.

12:17 Never pay back evil for evil.
Foresee what's good in all eyes.
12:18 If possible, be at peace with all
As far as within you lies.

12:19 Dear friends, do not seek revenge,
But unto God's wrath give way.
As it is written, "The Lord says,
'Vengeance is Mine. I'll repay.'"

12:20 If your foe has thirst, then quench it.
If he hungers, feed him bread,
For if you do this, you will pile
Burning coals upon his head.

12:21 So do not let what is evil
Conquer you; *it never should.
Instead, conquer all that's evil
With the instrument of good.

13:1 To the higher authorities,
Of government◆ *that is to say,
Let every soul submit himself.
Don't resist or disobey.[48]

For no authority exists
Unless by God *it's sustained,
And all of them that do exist,
By God they've been ordained.

13:2 So then, the person who resists
The authoritative seat
Stands opposed to what God's ordained,
And punishment they will meet.

13:3 For in regards to doing good,
Rulers aren't a tool of fear,
But rulers are a cause of fright
For bad behavior. *That's clear.

Now do you wish never to fear
Authority *in these days?
Practice the good, *never the bad,
And from them, you'll have the praise.

13:4 Because to you and for your good,
God's servant they have been made.
But if you do practice what's bad,
Then you had better be afraid.

For it is not without reason
That any carry the sword.
They're a tool of wrath on the bad.
They're a servant of the Lord.[49]

13:5 Therefore, to keep in submission
Is a priority to make,
Not just because of legal wrath[50]
But for your conscience' sake.

13:6 Because of this, pay taxes[51] too,
For God's servants of the state
Devote themselves to that same thing,
So them let's compensate.◆

13:7 Pay back what's owed to everyone,
All tax to whom tax is due,[52]
Honor to whom honor is owed,
Respect ◆and reverence too.

13:8 Owe nobody nothing at all,
Except this one, *no other,
Keep on loving unselfishly
Each sister and each brother.[53]

The person who loves his neighbor
Has truly fulfilled all law,
13:9 For out of several commandments*
There's one that we can draw.*

"Do not commit adultery,
And do not murder or steal,
Do not covet," and such commands
Can be summed in one ideal:

"To love your neighbor as yourself!"
13:10 And this love contains no flaw,*
Working no ill to a neighbor.
Therefore, love fulfills all law.

13:11 Do this since you know the season.
Wake now from sleep, you must.
For our salvation is nearer
Than when Christ we first did trust.

13:12 The nighttime has greatly progressed,
And the day, near it has drawn.
So, let's take off works of darkness,
And light's armor let's put on.

13:13 As in the day, let us then live,
Not in sin,* but decency,
No carousing or drunkenness
Or sexual impurity.

As in the day, yes, let us live,◆
Not in sin, but decency,◆
Not in wild and unbridled lust,
Or in strife or jealousy.

13:14 But put on the Lord Jesus Christ,
Not giving forethought one bit
For the flesh, ◆the sinful nature,
Its desires to commit.

14:1 Now continue on receiving
The ones who in faith are weak,
But not so that you can settle
Differences in how you speak.

14:2 On the one hand, one has the faith
That all things he can ingest.
On the other, the one who's weak,
Vegetables just are stressed.

14:3 Let not the one who eats all things
Despise him who eats no ◆meat,
And let not him who does abstain
Judge him who decides to eat.

For each of them God has received
As His own servant, *brother.
14:4 Just who are you so as to judge
The servant of another?

He stands or falls by His master
To whom he does belong.
And stand he will because the Lord
Can make him stand *without wrong.

14:5 And one person might judge a day
As above the other days.
Another one might judge each day
As equal in all ways.

Let each person be persuaded
Thoroughly in his own mind,
Whether it be about a day*
Or about food of some kind.*

14:6 The person who regards a day,
That day for the Lord he ranks.
The one who eats, eats for the Lord,
For to God, he does give thanks.

And the person who does not eat,
For the Lord, he does abstain,
And even though he does not eat,*
He gives thanks to God *the same.

14:7 For none of us lives for himself,
And for himself no one dies,
14:8 For if we live, it's for the Lord.
If we die, it is likewise.

Therefore, we belong to the Lord
If we die or if we live.
14:9 Christ died and lived for a reason,
Which reason I now will give.*

Christ died and lived to rule over
Both the living and the dead.
14:10 So, why do you judge your brother
Or pour contempt on his head?

For we'll all stand before the place
Where God's judgment seat does rest,
14:12 And each of us will of himself
Give account by what's confessed.

14:11 For just as it has been written,
"'I do live,' the Lord does stress,
'Because each knee to Me will bow,
To God each tongue will confess.'"

14:13 Therefore, let's not any longer
Be judging one another,
But rather you be judging this
In regards to your brother:

Judge that which is a stumbling block,
And judge that which is a snare,
And in the path of your brother
Don't put any of them there.

14:14 I know and am fully convinced,
In the Lord Jesus *I mean,
That there exists nothing at all
That in itself is unclean.

But to the one who ◆in his mind
Thinks something to be unclean,
Then to that one it surely is
Though by you it's not how it's seen.*

14:15 So then, if for the sake of food
Grief to your brother you're giving,
Then according to selfless love
You are no longer living.

Stop ruining by your own food
The one for whom Christ did die.
14:16 So, let not what is good for you
Be called a bad thing thereby.

14:17 For God's kingdom is not about
Eating or drinking but these:
The things that are in the Spirit,
Like righteousness, joy, and peace.

14:18 For he who serves Christ in this way,
Which way is firm and unmoved,*
That person is pleasing to God
And also by men approved.

14:19 Therefore, let us pursue the things
That in the Spirit◆ make peace
And that build up one another.
14:20 As for tearing down, let's cease.◆

Stop tearing down the work of God
Because of food anymore.
Though it's true that all foods are clean,
This truth we cannot ignore:*

If a person consumes a food,
Becoming a stumbling block,
Then as for him, eating that food
Is an evil way to walk.

14:21 So, it is good not to eat meat.
It is good not to drink wine.
It's good not to do anything
That makes your brother decline.[54]

14:22 The personal faith that you have,
Hold before God's *very eyes.
He's blessed who, in what he approves,
Himself does not criticize.

14:23 But if one eats with any doubt
Or hesitation within,◆
He stands condemned by lack of faith,
For what's not of faith is sin.

15:1 We who are strong must then support
The weaknesses of the weak,
And must not live to please ourselves.
Selfish living do not seek.◆

15:2 Let each of us please our neighbor
For his good, to edify,
15:3 For Christ did not please His own self
As the Scriptures testify.◆

For just as it has been written
In a psalm of prophecy,*
"The insults that they threw at You,
They have fallen upon Me."

15:4 Now all that was written before
Was for our education
In order that we might have hope
Through written exhortation.

The written Word called◆ the Scriptures,
Within us does inspire
Both patience and encouragement
So that hope we might acquire.

15:5 May God who gives encouragement
And patience *that has sufficed
Give you one mind with one another
According to Jesus Christ.

15:6 This is so that, as with one mouth,
You all might in one accord
Glorify the God and Father
Of Jesus Christ our Lord.

15:7 Therefore, receive one another,
Although imperfect and flawed,*
Just as also Christ received you
All for the glory of God.

15:8 I say, on behalf of God's truth
Christ served the circumcised
To confirm the Patriarchal oaths
That God Himself had devised.*

15:9 Christ also served the circumcised
So God would be glorified
By the Gentiles for His mercy
Which Scripture has testified.◆

For just as it has been written,
"Due to this I will confess
You, O Lord, among the Gentiles.
Your name I will sing *and bless."

15:10 Again it says, "Rejoice Gentiles.
With all God's people rejoice."
15:11 It says, "All Gentiles, praise the Lord.
Let all praise Him *in one voice."

15:12 And again as Isaiah says,
"From Jesse, the root will spring.
He'll arise to rule the Gentiles,
And their hope in Him will cling."

15:13 Now may the God who gives out hope
In the faith ◆you have in Him,
With every kind of peace and joy,
Fill you completely within.

And may the God of hope do this◆
For this purpose *that I write:
That you overflow with that hope
In the Holy Spirit's might.

15:14 I myself am fully convinced
About you all, my brothers,
You're full of good because you know
How to admonish others.

15:15 But in some things I've written you
With boldness so as to *prod,
Reminding you due to the grace
Which was given me by God.

15:16 As Jesus Christ's priestly servant
For the Gentiles, I do stand,
By ministering as a priest
The gospel from God's hand.

This is so that the offering
Of Gentiles be qualified
As one that is acceptable,
In the Spirit sanctified.

15:17 Therefore, in the presence of God
Boasting in Jesus[55] I air,
15:18 For what Christ has not done through me,
To speak that, I will not dare.

Gentiles became obedient
By my work and word conveyed
15:19 In the power of the Spirit
By signs and wonders displayed.

The results - from Jerusalem
Around to Illyricum,
I have preached the gospel of Christ,
So my preaching there is done.

15:20 To preach where Christ has not been named,
That is my concentration
So that I do not build upon
Another one's foundation.

15:21 As it is written, "Those to whom
The gospel did not extend,
The people who have never heard,
They'll see and comprehend."

15:22 Therefore, I was often hindered
From coming to you before,
15:23 But now in the regions mentioned
I have no place anymore.

Because I have had the desire
To see you for many years,
15:24 I hope I do by way of Spain
Whenever that moment nears.

And so when I am passing through
While on my journey to Spain,
After some enjoyment with you,
Your support I hope to gain.

15:25 But now up to Jerusalem
To serve the saints I must go.
15:26 Macedonia and Achaia
Were pleased their help to bestow.

To the poor Jerusalem saints
15:27 They supplied a donation,
Not just out of their good pleasure
But out of obligation.

Because with them the Gentiles share
In the spiritual concerns,
Likewise in the physical things
They're obligation turns.

15:28 Therefore, when this project I end
And to them I've sealed this fruit,
I'll begin my journey to Spain,
Coming to you on my route.

15:29 And whenever I do arrive,
I know *that this will be true:
In the fullness of Christ's blessing
I will come and visit you.

15:30 I urge by the Lord Jesus Christ,
Also by the Spirit's love,
That you strive with me in the prayers
For me to the God *above.

15:31 Pray with me that I be rescued
From the unbelievers' hands
Who are living in Judea,
And that my service stands.

For it is for Jerusalem.
So, pray with me ◆to this end,
That the saints accept my service
Which to them I will extend.

15:32 Pray so that when I come to you
In joy by means of God's will,
A restful time I'll have with you.
So, pray that this God fulfill.◆

15:33 And the one God, who gives His peace
To every believer, then,[56]
He is present with all of you,
And that is the truth.[57] Amen.

16:1 I recommend Phoebe to you,
Our sister *and a beacon.
She serves the church in Cenchrea
As a lady deacon.

16:2 I recommend for the purpose
That like this you'd receive her:
In the Lord and in a manner
That befits a believer.[58]

I recommend for the purpose◆
That you help her as she needs,
For to many, even to me,
She's a helper *in good deeds.

16:3 My coworkers in Christ Jesus
16:4 Who risked their necks for my life,
Please greet them, that is Aquila
And Prisca *who is his wife.

Gentile churches give thanks to them
And not only me alone.
16:5 Give greetings also to the church
Which gathers in their home.

Greet my dear friend, Epaenetus,
Who in Christ is the first fruit,
That is, in the Asian province.
He's the first Christian recruit.◆

16:6 Greet Mary who's toiled much for you.
Greet my fellow prisoners too,
16:7 Andronicus and Junia,
Each being a fellow Jew.

Both came to be in Jesus Christ
Long before I was in Him.
Also among the apostles
Outstanding they have been.

16:8 And greet my dear friend in the Lord,
Ampliatus, *as he's known;
16:9 Greet Urbanus who is in Christ
A coworker of our own.

Also, greet my dear friend Stachys,
16:10 And Apelles greet as well,
For he has been approved in Christ.
His character does excel.*

The house of Aristobulus,
Give greetings to them too.
16:11 And also greet Herodion
Who is my fellow Jew.

Greet all those who are in the Lord
Who to Narcissus belong.
16:12 Greet Tryphena and Tryphosa
Whose work in the Lord is strong.

Greet Persis who's worked much in Christ[59]
And who's well-loved *all the time.
16:13 Greet Rufus, chosen in the Lord,
Also his mother and mine.

16:14 Greet Asyncritus, and Phlegon,
And Hermes, and these others:
Patrobas, Hermas, and with them
Those who are our brothers.

16:15 Greet Philologus and Julia.
Greet also Olympas, then.
Greet Nereus and his sister
And all the saints with them.

16:16 And lastly greet one another
With a holy affection.
All the churches of Jesus Christ
Send greetings your direction.

16:17 Now I, brothers, am urging you
That on these your eyes be turned,
Those who cause strife and stumbling,
Contradicting what you've learned.

And keep away from all of them,
16:18 For our Lord Christ they serve not.
Instead, they serve so to fulfill
The appetites they have got.

And by their speech, which is so smooth,
Certain hearts they do deceive.
Through their eloquence, they draw in
The innocent and naïve.

16:19 For the report has spread abroad
About your obedience.
Because of that, I do rejoice
Over you *in that sense.

But I want you to gain wisdom
In things pertaining to good.
But in things pertaining to bad,
Stay innocent, *as you should.

16:20 The God of peace will crush Satan
Beneath your feet with all speed.
The grace that's from our Lord Jesus
Is with all of you, indeed!

16:21 Now Timothy, my coworker,
And these fellow Jews do too,
Lucius, Jason, Sosipater,
They send their greetings to you.

16:22 I, Tertius, greet you in the Lord,
I who this letter have penned.
16:23 Gaius, my host and the church's,
His greetings he does send.

The city treasurer greets you,
Erastus, *that is his name,
And last of all our brother here,
Quartus, he does the same.[60]

16:25 Now to the One who is able
To establish you in strength
In accordance with *these two things
Which I now explain at length:*

He is able to make you strong
According to my good news,
The proclaiming of Jesus Christ
To the Greeks and to the Jews.*

He is able to make you strong◆
According to this revealed:
The unveiling of the mystery
That in ages past was sealed.

It was sealed so not to be seen,◆
16:26 But now it has been made known.
By the writings of the prophets
The mystery has been shown.◆

The eternal God commanded
Prophets to write *in their day.
This is now shown to all nations
So by faith, they would obey.

16:27 To the one and only wise God
Who is unmatchable, then,*
Who is the glory forever
Through Jesus Christ. Amen.

THE POETIC FIRST LETTER TO THE CORINTHIANS

1:1 Paul, called to be an apostle
Of Christ Jesus by God's delight,
And Sosthenes who's our brother,
This epistle we now write.*

1:2 We write* to you, the church of God
Which in Corinth does reside,
You who are called as saints because
In Christ you've been sanctified.

Now you are saints along with those
Who in each and every place
Call on the name of Jesus Christ[61]
Who's Our Lord and theirs *by grace.

1:3 To all of you *I write these words:
Grace and peace on you are poured,[62]
Which proceed from God our Father
And from Jesus Christ the Lord.

1:4 To my God I render much thanks
All the time in your case
For the gift given you by God
In Christ Jesus, that is, grace.

1:5 This grace is that you were enriched
In Him in every way,
In all knowledge and all speech
1:6 As His witness does convey.◆

The testimony of Jesus
In you, found confirmation,
1:7 Resulting in no lack of gifts
As you wait in expectation.

Jesus Christ our Lord you await,
His appearance, *that's to say.
1:8 He'll confirm you until the end,
Without blame in our Lord's[63] day.

1:9 God is faithful *to do this thing.
You were called by that faithful One
Into fellowship with our Lord,
Jesus the Christ, His Son.

1:10 I urge you, brothers, in the name
Of Jesus Christ our Lord,
That you always speak the same,
And that there be no discord.

I urge you, brothers, in His name,◆
That you all be intertwined,[64]
Woven together◆ in one plan,
United in the same mind.

1:11 For it has been made clear to me
By those of Chloe's household
That, my brothers, among you all
Contentions are *manifold.

1:12 I mean, each of you by your words
Would have the church body sliced:*
"I'm of Paul"; I'm of Apollos";
"I'm of Cephas"; "I'm of Christ."

1:13 But think!* Has Christ been divided?
In your place, Paul was not slain
By being crucified, was he?
Were you baptized in Paul's name?

1:14 Thank God that Crispus and Gaius
Were the only ones I baptized,
And that by me none of you were
So that this would be realized:*

1:15 That none would say they were baptized
Into the name that I've got.
1:16 Oh, the household of Stephanas,
I baptized them. *I forgot.

As to the rest, I do not know
If I baptized any others,
1:17 For Christ sent me not to baptize
But to preach the gospel, *brothers.

I preach the gospel not in speech
Where my wisdom is applied
In order that the cross of Christ
Might not be nullified.

1:18 For to those who are perishing,
To those who reject the word,*
The reasoning about the cross
Is foolishness ◆and absurd.

But this is not the case *with all
Before whom the word is waved,*
For the gospel is God's power
To us who are being saved.

1:19 For it's written, "I will destroy
All the wisdom of the wise;
And all the intellectuals,
Their intellect I'll despise."

1:20 Where is the wise? Where is the scribe?
Where's the debater of this time?
Did not God take the world's wisdom
And to foolishness it assign?

1:21 For since in the wisdom of God
The world did utterly fail
To come to personally know[65] God
Through their wisdom *which they hail -

God Himself was utterly pleased
Through *a foolishness they perceive,
The foolishness of the message,
To save the ones who believe.

1:22 The Jews ask for some kind of sign,
And wisdom Grecians seek,
1:23 But we preach Christ as crucified
To the Jew and to the Greek.◆

To Gentiles Christ is foolishness,
To Jews, just a stumbling stone,
1:24 But to the called, both Jews and Greeks,
He's God's power and wisdom alone.

1:25 For God's foolishness is wiser
Than the wisdom men shower,
And God's weakness is much stronger
Than any human power.

1:26 For observe your calling, brothers,
That by standards of this earth
There weren't many wise or mighty,
Or many of noble birth.

1:27 God chose the foolish of the world
In order to shame the wise.
So as to shame the strong, God chose
Those weak in the world's eyes.

1:28 God chose the lowly and despised,
"The nothings" as the world deems,
So that He might bring to nothing
The things that the world esteems.

1:29 Thus, no flesh can boast before God,
1:30 For by Him *and Him alone
You yourselves are in Christ Jesus.
So no boasting can you own.[66]

Jesus Christ became to us all,
And this without exemption,*
Wisdom from God and righteousness,
Holiness and redemption.

1:31 Jesus is all these things to us*
To fulfill what's written down,
"Let the one who keeps on boasting,
In the Lord his boasting sound."

2:1 And when I came to you, brothers,
Preaching the mystery[67] of God,
I did not come with lofty words
Or with wisdom *to applaud.

2:2 For to know nothing among you,
I eagerly did decide,
Save the person of Jesus Christ
And that person crucified.

2:3 And I came to you in weakness,
In much trembling and in fear.
2:4 My speech and message weren't deemed wise,
Not persuasive *to the ear.

I came to display the Spirit
And His power in your sight
2:5 So that your faith would not find rest
In men's wisdom but God's might.

2:6 We speak wisdom with the mature
But not a wisdom of this day
Or a wisdom of its rulers
Who are just passing away.

2:7 We speak God's wisdom in this way:
In a long-hidden mystery,
Which God predestined for our glory,
Long before man's history.

2:8 By the rulers of this era
This mystery was not applied,[68]
For if it were, the Lord of glory
They would not have crucified.

2:9 "Eyes did not see, ears did not hear,
Neither did enter man's heart,
What God made for those who love Him."
The Scriptures to us impart.

2:10 But God revealed these things to us
By the Spirit ◆whose search is broad.
The Spirit searches everything,
Even the deep things of God.

2:11 For who is there among mankind
Who knows the things in a man?
Just the human spirit in him
Does know and understand.

So it's true with the things of God
No person can really know,
Just the Holy Spirit of God
Who searches to and fro.*

2:12 We didn't receive the world's spirit.
God's Spirit we did receive
So we might know the things that God
Gifted to us *who believe.

2:13 We also speak these things but not
In the words that have been taught
By the wisdom of humans. *No!
Such speech we have not brought.◆

But rather we speak all these things
In the words the Spirit has taught,
Explaining what is spiritual
By the spiritual *as we ought.

2:14 The natural man does not receive
The things of the Spirit of God,
For to him, they are foolishness.
Those things he will not applaud.*

It is not even possible
For him to have ever learned
The things of the Spirit of God
Since they're spiritually discerned.

2:15 But the spiritual man discerns
The spiritual things *he's taught,
And he himself is not discerned
By any person's thought.

2:16 Who has really known the Lord's mind
That he will be the Lord's guide?
We ourselves have the mind of Christ.
His Spirit in us does reside.[69]

3:1 To you as to spiritual ones
I was not able to speak,
But only as to fleshly ones,
As to babes in Christ. *You're weak.

3:2 I gave you milk, not solid food,
Because you could not yet eat.
Because you are still fleshly ones,
You still cannot eat meat.

3:3 Whenever there is among you
Envy and heated debate,
Are you not fleshly ones who live
According to mankind's state?

3:4 When one says, "I'm of Apollos,"
But another, "I'm of Paul,"
How are you not like mere mankind?
You are just like them, ◆you all!

3:5 So, what is Apollos really,
And what is Paul, I ask? -
Servants through whom you came to faith
As the Lord gave each a task.

3:6 I came along to plant *the church.
Apollos watered *the seed,
But God caused the growth *of the church.
He brought the increase, indeed.◆

3:7 So, what is the important thing:
Just who did water or sow?
Neither of them is anything,
Just God who caused all to grow.

3:8 The planter and waterer are one,
And each a reward will gain.
According to his own labor
A reward each will obtain.◆

3:9 For we are God's co-laborers.
You are God's field that is tilled.
You are also God's own building,
And all this as He has willed.*

3:10 According to the gift I have
Which was given by God's grace,
As a master builder who's wise,
A foundation I did place.

But upon this set foundation
Another builds to this day,
And every builder must observe
If he's building the right way.

3:11 Because another foundation
Cannot be possibly poured
Besides the one already set
Which is Jesus Christ *our Lord.

3:12 If one builds on this foundation,
Whether with silver or gold,
Or precious stones, logs, hay, or straw,
3:13 That person's work will unfold.

For each and every person's work
Will come into open view,
For on that day there will be shown
All of the works that are true.*

All of the works will be revealed
In a fire that will clearly prove
The quality of each one's work.
It will keep or it will remove.*

3:14 If anyone's work of building
On the foundation remains
After it passes through the fire,◆
A reward that one then gains.

3:15 If anyone's work of building
Becomes burnt up by the flame,
It will be lost, but as through fire.
His salvation will still remain.

3:16 Don't you know that as one body[70]
God's sanctuary are you,
Also that the Spirit of God
Dwells among your group? ◆It's true.

3:17 If any destroy that building,
God will destroy him as well.
God's sanctuary is holy,
Which you yourselves are, *I tell.

3:18 Let no person deceive himself.
If one is "wise" in this age,
Let him become a fool *for Christ
In order to be a sage.

3:19 For this world's wisdom is foolish
In the presence of God's eyes,
As it's written, "In their slyness
He catches them all, the wise."

3:20 There's more, "The Lord knows the thinking
Of the wise, that it is vain."
3:21 So, let no one boast in humans,
For all things are yours, *the same.

3:22 Yes, all things have been given you,◆
Whether Apollos or Paul,
Whether Cephas or the whole world,
These ones belong to you all.

Life or death, things now or future,
Or whatever God may give,*
3:23 All things are yours, and you are Christ's,
And Christ is God's. *So live.

4:1 Let a person in just this way
Regard us, *though we are flawed,
Both servants of Christ and stewards
Of the mystery of God.

4:2 In addition, it is required
For any steward, ◆it's a must,
That in that stewardship he'd be found
To be faithful over the trust.

4:3 Now it matters little to me
That I am being dissected
By you or by a human court.
As my judge, I'm not elected.

4:4 For I could judge myself and say,
"I'm guiltless," *and be aboveboard,
But that does not justify me.
My examiner is the Lord.

4:5 Now, therefore, stop passing judgment
Before the appointed season
Until the time the Lord returns
Who will judge with sound reason.*

He'll light up what hides in darkness.
The plans of the hearts He'll display,
And then by God the proper praise
Will be given each one that day.

4:6 Now these illustrations, brothers,
To myself, I have applied,
Also to Apollos as well.
For your sakes *these I've supplied.

This was done for the sole purpose
That in us you all might learn
What it means not to go beyond
What the Scripture does concern.[71]

This is so that no one at all
Become puffed up in a brother
To be leader of everyone,*
Choosing one against another.

4:7 Who distinguishes you, brother?[72]
Yourself how do you perceive?*
What exactly do you possess
That you never did receive?

You should know the answer to that.*
So, since you've truly received,
Why then boast as if you have not?
Only yourself you've deceived.*

4:8 You're already full of yourselves.
Already your wealth you did gain.
You already, and without us,
As kings have begun to reign.

I wish you really reigned as kings.
I wish that it were true,◆
For if you really reigned as kings,◆
We then could reign with you.

4:9 I think God has put on display
Us apostles as last of all,
As men who are condemned to death
Since to us, this did befall:

We, the apostles, have become
A spectacle to the world,
Not just to men but angels too.
To all we have been unfurled.*

4:10 We ourselves are just fools for Christ,
But you, in Christ you are wise;
We are just weak, but you are strong;
You're honored, but we're despised.

4:11 Even up to this present hour
We both hunger and we thirst;
We dress poorly and are homeless,
And we're treated as the worst.

4:12 We toil, working with our own hands;
When we're abused, we just bless;
When persecuted, we endure;
4:13 When slandered, we kindly address.

We have become just like garbage.
To the world, ◆we are just grime.
We've become the scum of all things
Even to the present time.

4:14 These things I am writing to you
Not to humiliate,
But as my dearly loved children,
To exhort *and motivate.

4:15 Even if your tutors in Christ
Number ten thousand *or more,
You do not have many fathers.
You as my children I bore.

In Christ Jesus through the gospel
I've given you birth, *you see.
4:16 Therefore, I urge that you become
Imitators of me.

4:17 For this reason to you I've sent
My dearly loved child in the Lord.
You have known him as* Timothy.
His faithfulness can't be ignored.

He will remind you of my ways,
My ways in Christ *which you know,
Just as in each and every church
I teach everywhere I go.

4:18 Now some of you became puffed up
As though I would never appear,
4:19 But soon I'll be coming to you.
To the Lord's will I'll adhere.

As to the prideful I will not come
To learn of their speech they spout,
But to learn of the power they have,
To learn what that's all about.*

4:20 For not in mere word but in power
God's kingdom does consist.
4:21 I'll come by rod or gentle love.
Which manner would you insist?

5:1 I hear, in actuality,
That among you there's been named
A kind of sexual impurity
Of which pagans are ashamed.

Specifically, that someone there
Is having his father's wife,[73]
Not his mother but step-mother.◆
What pagan parades that life?*

5:2 You yourselves are puffed up with pride,
And you should have mourned instead,
So as to remove from your midst
The man who defiled the bed.[74]

5:3 For I, though absent in body
But in my spirit right there,
As if I were really present,
Have already this to declare:*

In the name of the Lord Jesus
I've already judged the man
Who has produced this sinful deed.
Him from your midst you must ban.[75]

5:4 When you and my spirit with you
Are gathered in Jesus's power,
5:5 Deliver such one to Satan.
From this judgment do not cower.*

Deliver such one to Satan
For the flesh's ruination
So that in the day of the Lord
His spirit may have salvation.

5:6 Your boasting is not good at all.
Don't you realize, ◆don't you know
That just a little bit of yeast
Spreads through the whole lump of dough?

5:7 So that you become a new lump,
Clean out the old yeast *as God willed,
For you really are without yeast
Since our Passover, Christ was killed.

5:8 So let us celebrate the feast,
Not with the old leavened bread
That contains the yeast of evil
And wickedness that will spread.

But ◆let us celebrate the feast
With the new unleavened bread,
Described by truth and purity.
Let's celebrate this instead.*

5:9 I wrote to you in a letter
To never associate
With people who are immoral,
But let me elaborate.*

5:10 I did not mean the immoral
In the world ◆of unbelievers,
Like the ones who worship idols,
Or coveters and deceivers.

For if we all were to do this,
This world we would have to leave.
5:11 So, notice what I write you now
That this practice you receive.*

If someone is called a brother,
But in sinfulness does run,[76]
With him do not associate.
Don't even eat with such one -

Not one who gets drunk or reviles,
Or who swindles or fornicates,
Not the covetous or idolater,
Or any with such traits.*

5:12 For who am I to be the judge
Of those outside of "the Way"?[77]
Aren't you yourselves to be the judge
Of those on the inside, *I say?

5:13 Now God judges the outsiders.
So if there is evil within,
Remove it from among yourselves;
Remove the person of sin.◆

6:1 When in dispute with another,
Do some dare to go ahead
To be judged by unrighteous men
And not by the saints instead?

6:2 The saints will judge the world, ◆you know.
Or did you not know that fact?
So if the world be judged by you,
Why incompetence transact?◆

Are you all too incompetent
To make courts of low degrees?
6:3 Don't you know that we'll judge angels,
More so life's realities?

6:4 Therefore, if for this life's matters
There are courts that you have deemed,
Why then seat judges over you
Who in the church aren't esteemed?

6:5 I speak of this to your own shame.
Among yourselves can't you find
One who has the wisdom to judge
Between those of your own kind?

6:6 No! A brother with a brother
Goes to court to seek relief
And to be judged in the presence
Of those marked by unbelief.

6:7 Already it's a total loss
That you with yourselves have suits.
Why not just be wronged or cheated
Than to make legal disputes.*

6:8 But you yourselves are doing wrong;
You're cheating your own brother
When you go to unbelievers*
To judge between each other.*

6:9 Don't you know that the unrighteous,
God's kingdom won't inherit?
Do not keep on being deceived.
These sinners* will not share it:

Not the worshipers of idols,
Neither those who fornicate,
Not adulterers, effeminates,
Or the males who with males mate.

6:10 Not thieves, or the covetous,
Neither the ones who defraud,
Not the drunkards nor revilers
Inherit the kingdom of God.

6:11 Some of you were people like these,
But yourselves you purified;
But you were set apart *by God;
But you were justified.

And all this was done in the name
Of Jesus Christ the Lord,
And in the Spirit of our God
Who within us has been poured.*

6:12 All things are permitted to me,
But beneficial all are not.
All things are permitted to me,
But to slavery, I won't be brought.

6:13 Food is designed for the stomach,
And the stomach is for food,
But God will do away with both.
Be careful what you conclude.*

Now the body is not designed
To be sinful ♦and naughty,
But it is designed for the Lord,
And the Lord is for the body.

6:14 Now God raised the Lord from the dead,
And He'll raise us through His might.
6:15 Do you not know that your bodies
Are members of Christ? *That's right!

Therefore, do I just take away
Members of Christ and them make
To be parts of a prostitute?
By no means *in this partake!

6:16 He who joins with a prostitute
Is one body with her. Don't you know?
For "The two will become one flesh,"
Says *the Scripture from long ago.

6:17 But the one who joins with the Lord,
As one spirit they are glued.
6:18 Run away from fornication.
Its grasp you must elude.*

All sin is outside the body
Of the one who with sin shares,
But the person who fornicates,
Against his own body errs.

6:19 Or don't you know that your body
Is the Spirit's dwelling place,
The Holy Spirit who's in you,
Whom God gave you *by His grace?

You do not belong to yourselves,
6:20 For by a price you were bought.
Therefore, you must glorify God
In the body that you've got.

7:1 Now concerning the things you wrote,
Let's deal with marriage and such.*
It's good regarding a woman
That a man not sexually touch.

7:2 But due to immorality,
Each man should have his own wife
And each woman her own husband,
And that for a sexual life.*

7:3 Let the man fulfill to his wife
His sexual obligation.
Likewise, the wife to her husband
Make the same application.◆

7:4 The wife, over her own body,
Has no authority to wield.
The husband has authority
Over her body; *so yield.

The husband, over his body,
Has no authority to wield.
The wife has the authority
Over his body; *so yield.

7:5 Stop depriving one another
Unless you agree as a pair
That it be for just a season
To devote yourselves to prayer.

Then afterward come back again
And fulfill your marital role
So that Satan will not tempt you
Due to your lack of control.

7:6 Now I am not speaking all this
As a commandment to heed
But as a point so obvious*
That to it you would concede.

7:7 Now I wish that all people were
As even I am *this day,
But each has his own gift from God:
Like me or the other way.

7:8 To the singles and the widows
The following I convey:
For them to remain as I am
Is a good thing, I would say.

7:9 But if they don't have self-control,
Then let them marry; *they must.
It is much better to marry
Than it is to burn with lust.

7:10 To the married I do relay
These things the Lord wants enforced:
That a woman from her husband
Is not to become divorced.

7:11 But if she does, she must remain
Unmarried *for all her life,
Or be reconciled to her man,
And no man should divorce his wife.

7:12 Now to the rest of you I say
What the Lord did not address
About an unbelieving spouse*
That a believer might possess.*

If any brother has a wife
Who is an unbeliever,
If she agrees to live with him,
Don't allow him to leave her.

7:13 If any wife has a husband
Who in Christ◆ does not believe,
If he agrees to live with her,
Her husband, she must not leave.

7:14 For though the unbelieving man*
In unholiness does abide,*
In his wife, because she believes,
His marriage is sanctified.

For though the unbelieving wife*
In unholiness does abide,*
In her husband, ◆since he believes,
Her marriage is sanctified.

For if this were not really true,◆
Your children would be unclean.
So then, because this is the truth,
As holy they are seen.

7:15 But if the unbeliever leaves,
Then that one you must release.
In such cases, Christian's[78] aren't bound,
But God has called you in peace.

7:16 For who really knows, O woman,
If your husband you will save?
Or who knows if you'll save your wife,
O man, *you whom Christ forgave?

7:17 Only to each as the Lord assigned,
As God has called each *Christian,
Let each one live in that same state,
Whatever the condition.◆

And thus I direct all churches,
The churches in every place.◆
Was someone called when circumcised?
The marks let him not erase.

7:18 Was someone called to salvation
In an uncircumcised state?
Let him not seek circumcision,
For what would that demonstrate?*

7:19 Circumcision means not a thing,
Nor does uncircumcision.
Just the keeping of God's commands
Is the crucial condition.*

7:20 In the calling in which one was called,
In that condition remain.
7:21 Were you called while you were a slave?
No worry should you sustain.

But if you were saved as a slave*
And can also become free,
Then rather ◆than remain a slave,
Grab opportunity.

7:22 For if you were called while a slave,
In the Lord, you're His as freed.
Likewise, if you were called while free,
You're the slaves of Christ indeed.

7:23 You were purchased at a high price.
To men stop being enslaved.
7:24 Let each, brothers, stay before God
In that state in which he was saved.

7:25 Now concerning virgins, *brothers,
From the Lord, I've no command.
But as one trusted by His[79] mercy,
My opinion to you I hand.

7:26 I think, therefore, that it is good,
Due to the present distress,
For one to remain as he is;
Any change he should not press.*

7:27 Are you married to a woman?
Seek no release from that life.
Have you been released from marriage?
Stop trying to find a wife.

7:28 But even if you do marry,
You have committed no sin,
And if a virgin gets married,
No wrong has been done therein.

But those who don't heed my advice,
Added trouble you will bear
If you get married in these times.*
You I am trying to spare.

7:29 I mean to say this, my brothers:
This season's a shortened one,
And so all those who do have wives
Should live as if they had none.

7:30 And so all those who mourn should live
As if they had never wept.
And all those who rejoice should live
As if joy they had not kept.

And all those who make purchases
Should live as if what they bought
Were never in their possession,
Unconcerned with what they've got.*

7:31 Those who use the world's things should live
Without attachment *each day,
For the form of this present world
Is surely passing away.

7:32 Now from additional concerns
I wish for you to be free.
So let us compare the married*
To the single ones and see.*

About the matters of the Lord
A single man is concerned,
Thinking how he might please the Lord,
And so his mind is unturned.*

7:33 But about the things of this world
A married man is concerned,
Thinking how he might please his wife,
And so his mind has been turned.

7:34 The single woman is concerned
(And the virgin I include)
About the matters of the Lord,
Being in servitude.*

In her body and her spirit,
With a singleness of mind,*
She's concerned with being holy.
This in a wife we don't find.*

About the matters of this world
A wife makes herself concerned,
Thinking how to please her husband,
And so her mind has been turned.

7:35 Now I say this for your welfare,
Not to control any action,
But to show proper devotion
To the Lord without distraction.

7:36 If one thinks he's bringing disgrace
Against his virgin daughter
Who's well past the age of marriage
(I speak of him who begot her)-[80]

And if he surely ought to be
One no longer contrary,
Let him do just as he wishes.
He sins not. Let them marry.

7:37 But he who stands firm in his heart
Without receiving distress,
And possesses authority
His own wish ♦to impress -

The wish that he is determined
In his own heart *to excel,
Keeping his daughter a virgin -
In doing this he will do well.

7:38 So then, he who gives in marriage[81]
His virgin daughter does well,
Yet he who doesn't give in marriage
Will do better, *will excel.

7:39 As long as her husband lives,
A woman by law stands tied,
But if he falls into death's sleep,
The law is nullified.◆

So, she is free to be married
To whatever man she wills,
With one important restriction,
"In the Lord" *the man fulfills.

7:40 But as to my own opinion,
The widow would be much more blessed
If she would remain as she is.
With God's Spirit, I've addressed.

8:1 The next matter of which you wrote
Let us now briefly address:*
The things sacrificed to idols
And freedom one might express.[82]

Firsthand[83] knowledge about idols
All claim to have, we realize.
This kind of knowledge just puffs up,
But love is what edifies.

8:2 If one thinks to have known firsthand,
To be the authority,◆
That person did not really know
As he ought to know, *you see.

8:3 But if one keeps on loving God,
With unselfishness on display,[84]
That person has surely been known
By God in a personal way.

8:4 With this in mind, let us now deal
With the consumption of food,
The kind sacrificed to idols,
And how this should be viewed.*

Now we all know that an idol
In this world has no powers,
And we know that there is no god
Except for one, ◆and that's ours.

8:5 For though in heaven and on earth
There are gods that have been named,
As many gods and many lords
In this world are being claimed-*

8:6 But to us there is just one God.
He's the Father who does give
To all things their existence,
And for Him, we ourselves live.

And there's just one Lord, Jesus Christ,
Through whom all things came to be,
And we ourselves only exist
Through Jesus Christ's agency.

8:7 However, this firsthand knowledge
Does not exist among all.
But some, due to their past custom,
In the mind easily fall.◆

Even 'til now they eat as if
They have participated
In an offering to an idol,
Their weak conscience violated.

8:8 But food won't commend us to God
Whether we eat or abstain.◆
If we don't eat, we're not lacking.
If we eat, we do not gain.

8:9 Watch out that you do not become
To the weak a stumbling stone
By the freedom that you express
With a knowledge they've not known.

8:10 For if in an idol's temple
Some person sees that you dine,
Won't the conscience of one who's weak
To your freedom then resign?◆

Won't he be edified to eat
The food that is sacrificed
To an idol *as he used to
Before trusting Jesus Christ?*

8:11 For in this knowledge that you have
This one is not edified.*
Instead, he is being destroyed,
This brother for whom Christ died.

8:12 By sinning against your brothers,
Smiting their conscience that's weak,
You're really sinning against Christ
In this freedom that you seek.*

8:13 If food becomes to my brother
A stone to trip over, then,
So my brother may not stumble,
I'll never eat meat again!

9:1 Do I myself have a freedom?
Am I an apostle, no less?
Haven't I seen Jesus our Lord?
The answer to this is yes.[85]

You're my work in the Lord, aren't you?
9:2 Although I'm not to others
An apostle of Jesus Christ,
I'm one to you, *my brothers.

For as to my apostleship
Which the Lord conferred to me,
You are yourselves the very seal
Of its authenticity.

9:3 To those who just scrutinize me,
Hear my defense, *I plea:
9:4 We do not fail to have the right
To eat and to drink, do we?

9:5 Do we fail to possess the right
To take with us where we go
A wife who's a sister *in Christ?
The answer to this is no.[86]

All the rest of the apostles
Have this right. Why not us?
The brothers in the Lord have it,
And Peter known as* Cephas.

9:6 Or do just Barnabas and I
Have no authorization
Not to work *and be supported
By the Lord's congregation?*

9:7 What soldier is self-supporting
And his duties execute?
Or what farmer plants a vineyard
Without eating of its fruit?

Or is there a shepherd of a flock
That drinks not its milk? There's not!
9:8 I do not speak about these things
According to human thought.

Does not the Law write of these things?
9:9 For in Moses's Law it's plain:
"You are not to muzzle an ox
While it's treading on the grain."

God is not showing His concern
Just for the oxen, is He?
9:10 Or is God giving this command
To benefit you and me?

'Twas written for our benefit
Since he who plows ought to share
With the animal who threshes.
It is in hope they both fare.

9:11 If we sowed the spiritual things
For your benefit to keep,
Is it too much that we from you
Material things will reap?

9:12 If there are others who do share
This right over you to reap,
Surely we too should have this right,
But this right we did not keep.

This right we did not utilize,
But all things we do endure
So that to the gospel of Christ
No hindrance we might secure.

9:13 Those who work in the temple things
From it they eat, you're aware,
And those who serve at the altar,
In the altar they do share.

9:14 So, also the Lord commanded
Those who the gospel proclaim
That from the gospel ♦which they preach
Their living they sustain.

9:15 But I've not used any such rights,
And I write not for them to gain.
For me to die would be better
Than my boast to be in vain.

9:16 For when I proclaim the gospel,
About preaching I can't gloat
Since stress is being laid on me
For the gospel to promote.

Woe is me if I do not preach,
9:17 For if I preach by my choice,
I have a wage which I deserve.
Not so if I have no voice.*

For if I preach the gospel
Without the choice to declare,
I am given a stewardship,
Assigned to preach here and there.*

9:18 Therefore, what is my real reward?
That I preach not charging *a cent,
That my full right in the gospel
I would not implement.

9:19 For although in regards to all
I'm under no one's domain,
I enslave myself to them all
That more of them I would gain.

9:20 To a person who is a Jew,
To act as a Jew I choose.
In freedom I become enslaved*
So that I might gain more Jews.

To all those who are under law,
As under law I behave
(Although I am not under law)
So those under law I might save.

9:21 To all those who are without law,
Without any laws about sin,*
As one without law, I behave
So those without law I might win.

However, let me clarify,*
God's law I don't violate.
I myself behave lawfully
To Christ *to whom I relate.

9:22 I've become to the weak as weak
So that the weak might be won.
To all, I have become all things
That in them I might save some.

9:23 For all of the things which I do,
I do for the gospel's sake
So that I might become with it
A fellow who does partake.

9:24 Don't you know that in a stadium
All the runners run therein,
But only one receives the prize?
Run so the prize you'll win.

9:25 All competitors in all things
Are disciplined for this aim:
To gain a perishable wreath,
But we, one that will remain.

9:26 So I myself run in this way:
Having no uncertainty,
And I myself box in this way:
Without swinging aimlessly.

9:27 But my body I keep beating
In subjection as behooved
So that when I preach to others
I will not be unapproved.

10:1 So, my brothers, I do not want
Ignorance in you to be.
All our fathers were under the cloud,
And they all passed through the sea.

10:2 All were baptized into Moses,
In the cloud, and in the sea.
10:3 All ate the same spiritual food,
Which was manna, actually.*

10:4 All drank the same spiritual drink
Which from a rock was sent,
From the spiritual rock of Christ
That followed them as they went.

10:5 But God was not well pleased at all
With most of the people there,
For in the desert all were made
To be scattered everywhere.

10:6 But as an example to us
These things were *written and saved
So we would not long for evil
Just as evil they had craved.

10:7 Do not become idolaters.
As of them Scripture does say,
"The people sat to eat and drink,
And then they rose up to play."

10:8 Yield not to immorality,
The sexual kind, as some willed.
After they sinned, in just one day
Twenty-three thousand were killed.

10:9 And do not put Christ to the test.
This is repeating mistakes,*
For when some of them tested God,
They were destroyed by the snakes.

10:10 Do not spend your time murmuring,
For of meaning, it is void.*
What happened to those who murmured?
Them the destroyer destroyed.

10:11 All these things that happened to them
Were written to warn each one.
It's a lesson for us on whom
The ends of ages have come.

10:12 So then, watch out that you don't fall,
You who think that you stand.
10:13 No temptation have you received
Except what is common to man.

But the faithful God won't allow
Any temptation ◆or lure
To go beyond what you're able
To withstand or endure.◆

Because God will also provide
With each temptation ◆or lure
The pathway that will lead you out
So that it, you can endure.

10:14 For this reason, my dear brothers,
From idolatry run away.
10:15 I speak as to those who are wise.
Judge for yourselves what I say.

10:16 Is not the filled cup of blessing
For which we give thanks and bless
A sharing in the blood of Christ?
The answer to this is yes.[87]

Is not also the loaf of bread
Which we pass around and break
A sharing in the body of Christ?
Of course! ◆In Him, we partake!

10:17 Although we're made up of many,
And because one loaf we break,
We are one united body,
For from one loaf we partake.

10:18 Let us consider Israel,
I mean in the physical sense.
Aren't they who eat sacrifices,
In the altar participants?

10:19 In light of this, am I saying
That the sacrificial meal
To an idol has importance
Or that the idol is real?

10:20 No! The things that are sacrificed
Are to demons not to God.
I don't want you to be sharers
With that demonic squad.

10:21 You cannot drink from the Lord's cup
And the cup of demons too.
You cannot share the Lord's table
And that of demon's; *it's true!

10:22 Or are we daring to provoke
The Lord to jealousy?
We most assuredly are not
Stronger than Him, are we?

10:23 All lawful things are not helpful,
Nor do they all edify.
10:24 Let no person seek his own good,
But another's satisfy.

10:25 Eat all that's in the marketplace
Without investigation
For the sake of human conscience,
Avoiding violation.*

10:26 For as to what we eat or drink,*
This Scripture from Psalms pertains:*
"The earth belongs to the Lord
And everything it contains."

10:27 Let's assume some unbeliever
Invites you to eat a meal,
And let's assume you want to go.
Do not make food a big deal.*

Everything the unbeliever
Places before you to partake,
Eat without asking what it is
For the human conscience' sake.

10:28 But if someone were to tell you,
"This is sacrificial meat,"
For the sake of him who told you
And for conscience sake, don't eat.

10:29 Now I don't mean your own conscience
But the conscience of a brother,[88]
For why should my freedom be judged
By the conscience of another?

10:30 If I myself share in a meal,
Viewing the food◆ as God's grace,
Why should I, for that which I give thanks,
Be blasphemed in this case?

10:31 Therefore, whether you eat or drink,
Or any category,◆
Whatever you happen to do,
Do everything for God's glory.

10:32 Become people without offense
To those who are Greeks or Jews,
Or to those of the church of God.
To offend never choose.◆

10:33 I please all people in all things.
My own good I do not crave,
But just the good of the many
That some of them I might save.

11:1 Become imitators of me
In all that I've been stating,*
And you all will do very well*
Since Christ I'm imitating.

11:2 I praise you that in everything
Me in your mind you've retained,
And that you hold the traditions
Which to you I have explained.

11:3 Now I wish you to know some facts
Concerning authority:*
Christ is the head of every man,
Giving Christ priority.*

The head of woman is the man,
And the head of Christ is God.
Therefore, in your public meetings*
This order you must applaud.*

11:4 Each man who prays or prophesies
In a church or public place,*
And does it with his head covered,
Puts his own head to disgrace.

11:5 Each woman who prays or prophesies
With head uncovered ◆and bare,
Shames her head, for she is the same
As one who's shaved off her hair.

11:6 For if a woman does not have
Her head covered *as she should,
She might as well cut off her hair,
But this action is not good.*

So if it is a shameful thing
To have no hair above her
By cutting or shaving it off,
Then the head she must cover.

11:7 His own head to keep uncovered,
Each man is obligated
Since he's God's image and glory.
For this he was created.*

But the woman is man's glory,
11:8 For as Scripture does persuade*
That man did not come from woman,
But from man, woman was made.

11:9 Even so, take note in Scripture*
That incomplete man began.*
He was not made for woman,
But woman was made for man.

11:10 Because of this a woman must
A sign of authority take
And place it over her own head
For the angels' sake.[89]

11:11 However, in the Christian realm,[90]
Although there's ascendency,*
Woman and man need each other;
There's interdependency.

11:12 For the woman is from the man,
Yet the man can only survive
Through the woman *by means of birth,
But from God, all things derive.

11:13 Among you all judge for yourselves.
Is it proper *to display
A woman with head uncovered
Who stands before God to pray?

11:14 Does not even nature itself
Teach you concerning this case:
That if a man has long hair,
To him it brings disgrace?

11:15 But if a woman has long hair,
It is her glory ◆and pride
Since it is a covering for her
Which to her has been supplied.

11:16 Now if someone is contentious,
Deeming this argument flawed,*
We don't have another custom,
Nor do the churches of God.

11:17 Now in this charge I praise you not:
That you gather together
For a purpose that is harmful
Instead of for the better.

11:18 For when you gather as a church,
By the report I've received,
Among you divisions exist,
And this I've partly believed.

11:19 For it's also necessary
Among you to have factions
So that the approved among you
Might become the attractions.

11:20 Therefore, when you come together,
Gathering at the same place,◆
It is not in order to eat
The supper of the Lord's *grace.

11:21 For each one takes his own supper,
Not waiting for others to dine,◆
So that there are those who hunger
And those who are drunk with wine.

11:22 For don't you have your own houses
In which to drink and to eat?
Or God's church do you belittle
And shame those who have no meat?

What words should I speak to you all?
What kind of words should I phrase?◆
I will not speak highly of you.
In this, I do not praise.

11:23 For what I received from the Lord
I handed over to you:
The night in which He was betrayed
He told us what we should do.*

The Lord Jesus reached for a loaf,
11:24 Gave thanks, broke it, and then said,
"Eat this in remembrance of Me.
It's My body in your stead."

11:25 Likewise He took, after eating,
The cup and gave this decree:
"This cup is the new covenant
In My blood. Remember Me."

11:26 For as often as you partake
In the meal *with true concerns,
You proclaim in this bread and cup
The Lord's death 'til He returns.

11:27 So then, whoever eats the bread
And drinks the Lord's cup carefree,
Of the Lord's body and His blood
Guilty that one will be.

11:28 But let each one look at himself
Until all has been sufficed,[91]
And then let him eat from the loaf
And drink from the cup *of Christ.

11:29 For the one who drinks from the cup
And eats from the loaf of bread
Without discerning the body,
Brings judgment upon his head.

11:30 Due to this failure to discern,
God's judgment has been applied.*
Some of you are weak and sickly,
And a good number have died.[92]

11:31 But if we'd keep looking within,
Discerning ourselves rightly,
We would not be under judgment
Which no one should take lightly.*

11:32 But when we are judged by the Lord,
His discipline we receive
So that we will not be condemned
With those who do not believe.[93]

11:33 So then, my brothers, as you gather
In the same place of meeting,[94]
Wait patiently for each other,
And then begin your eating.[95]

11:34 If one comes with such a hunger
That he cannot wait to eat,
Let that one have a meal at home
So for judgment you won't meet.

As to the rest of the matters,
To you I will have to come
And give you verbal instruction
So as to resolve each one.*

12:1 Now another matter, brothers,
I have to address with care.*
Concerning the spiritual gifts,
I don't want you unaware.

12:2 You know that when you were pagans,
You were being led astray
To idols that could speak no words,
However you went that way.

12:3 So, these words I make known to you
That in them you'll be well versed:*
No one speaking in God's Spirit
Declares, "Jesus is accursed."

No one has the ability
To declare, "Jesus is Lord."
Only in the Holy Spirit
Are we brought to this accord.*

12:4 Now assortments of gifts exist,
Spiritual gifts, that's to say.◆
However, in each of the gifts,
The same Spirit *is on display.

12:5 And there are many ministries.
Varieties *we've observed.
Yet in all of these ministries
The same Lord *is being served.

12:6 And in the workings of these gifts
Variety does abound,
But the same God works all of them
Among people all around.

12:7 To each one receiving a gift,
The Spirit's manifestation
Is being given for the good
Of all in participation.*

12:8 For to one is being given,[96]
Through the Spirit's design,
A message that's characterized
By wisdom *that's divine.

However, to another one
A word of knowledge *divine
Is being given according to
That same Spirit's design.

12:9 To someone else the same Spirit
Gives faith *that is revealing;
Through another the one Spirit
Operates gifts of healing.

12:10 To another, miraculous works;
To another, prophecy;
To another, as to spirits,
A discerning ability.

To someone else, speaking in tongues,
Having no education;[97]
To another, as to those tongues,
Its interpretation.

12:11 But the one and the same Spirit
Works all these gifts and divides
To each one individually
Just as He decides.[98]

12:12 Our one body has many parts,
But although many, they're spliced
Into the body which is one.
So also it is with Christ.

12:13 For in one Spirit we were baptized
Into one body, *our link.
Whether Jews or Greeks, slaves or free,
In one Spirit we did drink.

12:14 For of not just a single part
Is the body comprised,
But of parts that are numerous.
That's the way it is devised.*

12:15 Suppose the foot were to reason,
"Because I am not a hand,
I am not part of the body."
Would the foot's reason then stand?

12:16 And if the ear were to reason,
"Because I am not an eye,
I am not part of the body."
Would that reason then apply?

12:17 If the whole body were an eye,
From where would the hearing come?
If the whole body were an ear,
How would the smelling be done?

12:18 But it is a matter of fact
That the parts God has assigned,
Each of the parts in the body,
Just as He wished *and designed.

12:19 But if all were only one part,
Then where would the body be?
12:20 But indeed there are many parts
Yet one body *obviously.

12:21 The eye cannot say to the hand,
"I don't have a need for you,"
Nor can the head say to the feet,
"I don't need *foot one or two."

12:22 But even more, the body parts
Which seem weaker than the rest
Are absolutely essential
For the body to function best.*

12:23 And the body parts which we deem
To lack honor, we esteem,
For our unpresentable parts
We care for to the extreme.

12:24 But for our presentable parts
This care is not essential.
God joined the parts to give what lacks
Treatment preferential.

12:25 God joined the body in this way
So schism would be nowhere,
But so the parts to one another
Would give equivalent care.

12:26 If one part happens to suffer,
Then all parts sympathize;
If one part happens to be praised,
Then all parts rejoice likewise.

12:27 Now all of you are Christ's body,
Together, that is to say,
And each and every one of you
Is one part of that array.

12:28 God has assigned within the church
An order that must be heard:*
Apostles first, prophets second,
And then those who teach are third.

Next, the working of miracles,
Then healing gifts ◆He's assigned,
Then helps and administrations,
And tongues of every kind.

12:29 Are all the people apostles?
Are they all prophets of God?
Are they all teachers of the word
Or do miracles *abroad?

12:30 Do all have the gifts of healing?
Or speak in tongues *they've not learned?
Are all able to interpret?
That's a "no" for all concerned.[99]

12:31 But be zealous for spiritual gifts,
The greater gifts, *that's to say,
And yet I now show to you all
A much superior way:

13:1 If I keep on speaking in tongues,
Tongues that I have not known,*
Human tongues or angelic ones,
But selfless love[100] is not shown -

What then have I really become*
But noise annoyingly strong.*
I've become a crashing cymbal
Or even a noisy gong.

13:2 And if I have a prophecy,
And all the mysteries I know,
And if I have all the knowledge,
And even all faith to show –

If I have all the faith needed
So as to make mountains fall,
But I do not show selfless love,
I'm really nothing at all.

13:3 If I give away all I owned,
Or give up my body to boast,
But did not have unselfish love,
There is no profit to post.

13:4 Unselfish love patiently waits;
In kindness it does *not lag;
It does not boil with jealousy;
About self, it does not brag.

Unselfish love is not puffed up;
13:5 It does not act in disgrace;
It does not seek its own interests;
To be provoked is not its face.

It does not keep records of wrong;
13:6 It does not ever rejoice
Over any unrighteousness,
But celebrates with truth's voice.

13:7 In spite of all circumstances,
Selfless love keeps protecting.
It keeps trusting, keeps enduring,
And in hope keeps expecting.

13:8 Selfless love never ever fails.
Prophecies will come to naught.
Tongues will eventually cease.
To an end, knowledge will be brought.

13:9 For incompletely we now know,
And we prophesy in part.
13:10 But whenever the perfect comes,
The partial will then depart.

13:11 When a child, I talked like a child.
Like one I reasoned and thought,
But when I grew into a man,
The childish I brought to naught.

13:12 For now we look in a mirror
That's an obscure reflection,
But then we will see face to face
When there arrives perfection.◆

Now we only know partially,
But then we will surely know
Just as we have been known *by God,
Fully and completely so.*

13:13 So, these three forever remain
Even after all gifts cease:*
Faith, hope and selfless love - and love,
It's the greatest of these.

14:1 Keep on pursuing selfless love,
Yet zeal earnestly apply
To spiritual gifts, but more so
In order to prophesy.

14:2 For the one who speaks in a tongue
Speaks not to people but God.
None understands since in spirit
Only mysteries he has jawed.[101]

14:3 But as for him who prophesies,
To people is that oration,
Speaking words of encouragement,
Comfort, or edification.

14:4 The one who just speaks in a tongue,
Himself that one edifies,
But the church is being built up
By the one who prophesies.

14:5 Now I want you to speak in tongues
But even more to this end:
In order that you prophesy
So that all will comprehend.*

Greater is he who prophesies
Than the ones who in tongues talk,
Unless one interprets the tongue,
Thus edifying the flock.[102]

14:6 But now, brothers, if before you
Speaking in tongues I come,
What benefit will I bring you
Unless understanding is won?

I must speak in divine knowledge,
Or in a revelation,
In a prophecy, or a teaching
In my communication.*

14:7 Even things that are without life
Are made to produce a noise,
Whether it be a flute or harp
Whose melody one enjoys.*

But if they were not to produce
A distinct melodic tone,
How then will what is being played
On the flute or harp be known?

14:8 For what if a trumpet sounded
In a tone that was unclear,
What person would prepare himself
For the battle *coming near?

14:9 So also, unless you produce
Through the tongue a distinct word,
How will the talk be understood?
Your speech would be absurd.[103]

14:10 It so happens that in the world
That languages just abound,
And none speaking any of them
Speak a nonsensical sound.

14:11 If I, therefore, don't know the sense
A person is trying to proclaim,
To that one, I'll be a babbler,[104]
And to me, they'll be the same.

14:12 Because, as to spiritual gifts,
You've got zealous elation,
Keep seeking so as to abound
In church edification.

14:13 Therefore, let the person who speaks
In a tongue *he does not know
Pray that the interpretation
Upon him God would bestow.*

14:14 If I pray in a tongue unknown,
My spirit prays *without dispute.
However, in understanding
My mind is without fruit.

14:15 Therefore, what is the thing to do?
In spirit, I'll pray and sing,
But I will also do the same
In my understanding.

14:16 For if you just praise in spirit,
What then will be the effect*
On the one who comes among you
So as the faith to inspect?[105]

How then will he say the "Amen"
Based upon your praying
When he is not able to know
Anything you are saying?

14:17 For you're giving thanks well enough.
Your praise cannot be denied,◆
But the one who's visiting you
Is not being edified.

14:18 I speak in tongues more than you all,
And I thank God that I do.
14:19 But in the church I wish to speak
In known words, even though few.

To speak five intelligent words
So I may instruct others
Is better than ten thousand words
In a strange tongue, my brothers.

14:20 So, stop becoming as children
Which in childish thinking results,
But in evil be like infants.
In your thinking be adults.

14:21 It has been written in the Law,
"In tongues which they have not known
And by other lips, I will speak
*To this people *of My own.*

"And even though I speak this way
*To these people who are Mine,**
They'll not even listen to Me,
Says the Lord *God divine."

14:22 Therefore then, tongues are for a sign
(The gift of tongues we've discussed),*
A sign not to him who has faith
But to him who does not trust.

Prophecy is not for a sign
(Unlike the tongues just discussed),*
A sign to him who has no faith
But to him who has true trust.

14:23 So, if everyone in the church
Were to gather in one place,
And each one was speaking in tongues,
What would occur in this case?*

What if outsiders entered in,
Those not trusting in His name,
How will they respond to your speech?*
Will they not say you're insane?

14:24 But if everyone prophesies
And somebody enters in,
Some unbeliever or outsider,
What then would happen to him?*

He would be convicted by all.
By all his judgment he'd hear.
14:25 The things he's hidden in his heart
Would be revealed *to his ear.

And so he would then worship God
By falling down on his face,
And then he would proclaim to all,
"God is truly in this place."

14:26 Therefore, my brothers, what's to be?
When you're a congregation -
Each one has a psalm, a teaching,
And a revelation.

Or each one has a tongue to speak
And an interpretation -
Make certain everything is done
To bring edification.

14:27 If one person speaks in a tongue,
Or two, or at the most three,
Let each one go ahead and speak,
But in turn, separately.

There must be an interpreter,
14:28 But if not, *do not prod.
Let him be silent in the church
And speak to himself and God.

14:29 And let two or three prophets speak,
Each one arising in turn,[106]
And let all the other prophets
Judge the message and discern.

14:30 But if some message is revealed
To another who is seated,
Let the first person keep quiet
'Til the message is completed.*

14:31 For all of you are capable
To prophesy each in turn
So that all may be encouraged,
And so everyone may learn.

14:32 And the spirits of the prophets
Are in subjection, *of course,
To the other prophets present,
Keeping all order in force.*

14:33 For God is not disorderly.
He's a God of peace *at heart,
As is true in all the churches
Of those who are set apart.

14:34 Let wives keep silent in the church,
For they're not allowed to chat,[107]
But let them be in subjection,
For the Law itself says that.

14:35 Now if they keep wanting to learn
Something *they have not known,
Let them have the habit of asking
Their own husbands at home.

It's shameful for a wife to chat
When in the church it is done.
14:36 Or did God's word derive from you?
Or to just you did it come?

14:37 If one thinks he is a prophet
Or a gift on him is poured,
Let him recognize what I write
As the commands of the Lord.

14:38 Now if someone keeps ignoring
Anything I've said before,[108]
That person, do not acknowledge.
That person, you must ignore.◆

14:39 So, for prophecy boil with zeal.
Speaking in tongues don't prevent.
14:40 Let all things be done decently
To an orderly extent.

15:1 Now, brothers, I reacquaint you
With the gospel you affirmed,
The gospel that I preached to you,
The good news as it's termed.◆

In this gospel, you firmly stand.
15:2 Through it you were saved *from blame
If you keep hold of what I preached,
Or else you believed in vain.

15:3 For I handed over to you
What was of highest concern,
The same thing that I had received,
The gospel which you did learn.◆

That is, that Christ died for our sins
As the Scriptures did record,
15:4 That He was buried *in a tomb,
But life to Him was restored.◆

That He's been raised since the third day
Just as the Scriptures had said,
15:5 That the Lord was seen by Cephas,
Then by the Twelve ◆as not dead.

15:6 Then He was seen at the same time
By more than five hundred brothers,
Most of which are alive today.
In death's sleep are the others.

15:7 Next was James, then all apostles
Who saw the Lord *on this earth.
15:8 Last of all He was seen by me
As one of untimely birth.

15:9 For I'm least of the apostles.
To be called one I'm unfit
Since God's church, I persecuted,
But His grace, it did acquit.*

15:10 By God's grace I am what I am.
It was not vain in my case,
But I toiled more than all of them,
I along with God's grace.

15:11 So, whether it was I or them
Who preached the word you received,*
We all proclaim it the same way,
And that message you believed.

15:12 Now if Christ is being proclaimed
That He's been raised from the dead,
How are some among you saying
The opposite instead?*

"Rising from death does not occur,"
Certain among you have phrased.
15:13 But if there's no resurrection,
Not even Christ has been raised.

15:14 And so if Christ has not been raised,
Our preaching is empty indeed,
And your faith is also empty
Since Christ then did not succeed.*

15:15 And we also are being found
As false witnesses of God
Since we testified against Him
A word that's just a façade.*

Namely, that God raised Christ from death
Whom He did not really raise
If there is no resurrection,
If the dead stay dead always.*

15:16 For if the dead are never raised,
Not even Christ came alive.
15:17 And so, if Christ has not been raised,
Your faith, *how can it survive?

Your faith is completely worthless.
You all are still in your sins,
15:18 And those who fell asleep in Christ
Have perished *because death wins.

15:19 If it is only in this life
That our hope in Christ we post,
Then of all the ones in the world
We're to be pitied the most.

15:20 Now *let's get back to the real truth.
Christ has been raised from the dead
As the first fruits of believers
Who've gone to sleep *in death's bed.

15:21 For since through a man death has come,
So too through a man, there'll come
The resurrection from the dead,
Applying to all, not some.*

15:22 For in Adam all people die,
And as with them, this is true,
So also all people in Christ
To life again will renew.

15:23 But each one in his own order:
Christ, the firstfruits, *came alive,
Then all those who belong to Christ
In His coming *will revive.

15:24 Then comes the end when the kingdom
To Father God, He'll submit,
When rule, authority, and power
He's abolished - all of it.

15:25 For He must reign 'til all His foes
Are put underneath His feet,
15:26 The last enemy being death
To be removed from its seat.

15:27 For hear this quote:* "He subjected
All things underneath His feet."
So what does He mean by all things?
He cannot Himself unseat.*

This excludes Him who subjected
All things to Christ. That's plain.
15:28 And when all things are under Christ,
Under God, He will remain.

The Son Himself will always be
Under the Father, as we call,[109]
Who subjected all things to Him
So that God might be all in all.

15:29 So, now that we've dealt with the truth*
Just what will those people do,
The ones who baptize for the dead?
Their actions don't match their view.*

For since they believe that the dead
Will never actually raise,
Then why baptism for the dead
Do they make part of their ways?

15:30 And why do we then put ourselves
In danger every hour?
15:31 By my pride for you in the Lord,[110]
I daily face death's power.

15:32 If I fought beasts in Ephesus
On human philosophy,
What benefit would I derive?
It would not benefit me.◆

You see,* if the dead are not raised,
This thought would better apply:*
"Let us all eat and let's all drink,
Because tomorrow we die."

15:33 Stop being deceived by reasoning
That speculate on the dead.[111]
"Bad company spoils good morals."
Therefore, stop being misled.

15:34 Rightly regain all your senses.
Stop giving in to sin's game,
For some have an ignorance of God.
I say this to your shame.

15:35 But someone will say, "Tell me now,
How the dead to life revert?
What sort of body will they have
When they come out ◆from the dirt?"

15:36 How foolish! Think of what you sow.
The seed is not made alive
Unless it dies, ◆decomposes,
And then it begins to thrive.◆

15:37 And what you sow, you do not sow
The body which is to be,
But a bare seed, perhaps of wheat
Or something else, *you see.

15:38 But God gives the seed a body
According to His wish alone,
And He gives each one of the seeds
A body of its own.

15:39 Now, not all flesh is the same flesh.
There is one of humanity,
One of beasts, another of birds,
And another of fish, *you see.

15:40 Heavenly and earthly bodies
Possess glory *of great worth,
But that of the heavenly ones
Differ from those of the earth.

15:41 There is one glory of the sun.
The moon has another kind,
And stars have a different glory,
Each star its own assigned.

15:42 The resurrection from the dead
Is also like what's been phrased.
In corruption, the body's sown.
Without corruption, it's raised.

15:43 In dishonor the body's sown,
But raised to a glorious state.
In weakness, the body is sown,
But raised in a strength that's great.

15:44 It is sown a natural body.
That's a mortal condition.*
It's raised a spiritual body[112]
Without decomposition.*

If there is a natural body
Which will just rot and decay,*
There too is a spiritual one
Which we will receive one day.[113]

15:45 So we read, "The first man, Adam,
Became a being that lives."
The last Adam is a spirit,
And life is what He gives.

15:46 But the spiritual is not first,
As deemed by the Creator.*
The natural is first in order.
The spiritual comes later.

15:47 The first man, consisting of dust,
From the earth, he was designed.
The second man came from heaven
In order to save mankind.*

15:48 As is Adam, the earthy man,
The earthy ones are as much.
As is Christ, the heavenly Man,
The heavenly ones are such.

15:49 And just as we bore the image
Of the earthy man *at birth,
We'll bear the image of the Man
Who came from heaven *to earth.

15:50 In plain words, as to God's kingdom
Flesh and blood can't inherit.
To be heir of incorruption,
Corruption cannot share it.

15:51 Behold I tell you a mystery.
We believers won't all fall
Into the slumber of death's grip,
But changed we will be, yes all!

15:52 It will happen in an instant,
In the blink of an eye – *that fast,
And it will happen in the day
Of the final trumpet blast.

For the final trumpet will sound,
And then will be raised the dead,
Having no corruption at all,
And we'll be changed, *as I've said.

15:53 For this body that is corrupt
Must out of necessity
Receive what's incorruptible
To wear for eternity.

And this body that is mortal
Must out of necessity
Receive that which is immortal
To wear for eternity.

15:54 When the aforementioned occurs,[114]
This word, *which is prophecy
Written *in the holy Scriptures,
Will be a reality:

15:55 "Death was completely swallowed up
Into victorious might.
O death where is your victory?
O death now where is your bite?"

15:56 Now realize that sin's bite is death.
Through the Law, it worked its power.
15:57 But thank God through our Lord Jesus Christ
Who on us, victory did shower.

15:58 So then, my beloved brothers,
Stand firm and in strength remain.
Always excel in the Lord's work,
Since you know it's not in vain.

16:1 Now concerning the collection
For the Jerusalem[115] saints.
What I told the Galatian churches,
You do *without complaints.

16:2 On the first day of every week
Let each of you set aside,
Saving something from what you earned
For the need to be supplied.

This is so that, when I arrive,
There'll be no collections made.
16:3 Now whenever I do arrive,
The sending will not be delayed.*

I will send official letters
With the people that you choose
To carry to Jerusalem
Your gift *for the saintly Jews.

16:4 Now if it be appropriate
That I make this trip as well,
Then they will accompany me
As your chosen personnel.*

16:5 And as for Macedonia,
When I finish passing through
(For this is the way I'm going),
I will certainly come to you.

16:6 But, perhaps, I will stay with you
Or even spend winter there
In order that you may send me
Whenever I go elsewhere.

16:7 For I don't wish to see you now
Merely as I'm passing through,
For I hope, if the Lord allows,
To stay for some time with you.

16:8 But I'll remain in Ephesus
Until Pentecost. Here's why.
16:9 A wide, useful door stands open,
And many people defy.

16:10 See that Timothy feels no fear
Whenever he comes to you,
For he does the work of the Lord
Even as I also do.

16:11 Therefore, let no one despise him.
In peace send him back to me,
For his return with the brothers
I await expectantly.

16:12 As for our brother, Apollos,
I encouraged him a lot
To come to you with the brothers,
But willing he was not.

Even now he is unwilling,
But somewhere along the line*
He'll eventually come to you
When there's an opportune time.

16:13 Keep watching by being on guard.
In the faith keep standing long.
16:14 Let all be done with selfless love.
Act like men by staying strong.

16:15 Stephanas's house are the first fruits
Of Achaia, as you've noted,
And for the service to the saints,
Themselves they have devoted.

So, brothers, I encourage you
16:16 To these be in submission,
Also to all who work with us
And labor *with ambition.

16:17 In Stephanas, Fortunatus,
And Achaicus I rejoice
Because these men came and supplied
What you lacked *though not by choice.

16:18 For they have refreshed my spirit
As yours, they've refreshed as well.
So, acknowledge personally
Such men *who in deeds excel.

16:19 The churches of Asia greet you.
Aquila and Prisca *his spouse
Greet you warmly in the Lord
With the church inside their house.

16:20 All the brothers give their greetings.
Greet all with a holy kiss.
16:21 I Paul, give my greeting to you.
With my own hand, I write this.

16:22 If someone does not love the Lord,
Possessing no affection,[116]
Let that one be anathema,
Accursed, without connection.[117]

Maranatha! Lord Jesus come![118]
16:23 His grace is with you,[119] *I tell.
16:24 My love which is in Christ Jesus
Is present with you as well.

THE POETIC SECOND LETTER TO THE CORINTHIANS

1:1 Paul, an apostle belonging to
Christ Jesus by God's delight,
And the brother called Timothy,
This epistle we now write.*

We write* to you, the church of God
Which in Corinth does reside,
Along with all the saints of God
Who throughout Achaia abide.

1:2 To all of you I write these words:*
Grace and peace on you are poured[120]
Which proceed from God our Father
And from Jesus Christ the Lord.

1:3 Blessings to the God and Father
Of Jesus Christ our Lord.
He is the Father of mercies
From whom all comfort is poured.

1:4 In all of our tribulation
He brings comfort to us all,
So that we can comfort those
Who in tribulation fall.

It matters not what kind it is,◆
For the comfort which we bring
Is the same we received from God.
We can comfort in anything.

1:5 For just as the sufferings of Christ
Us abundantly surround,
Similarly through Jesus Christ
Our comfort does abound.

1:6 If we're oppressed, it is for you,
Your comfort and salvation.
When we're comforted in our woe,
It's for your consolation.

When you suffer as we've suffered
(I say this to reassure),*
You will have our same comfort
Which will move you to endure.

1:7 Our hope for you is firm because
As in our suffering, you share,
So you'll also partake with us
In comfort *to help you bear.

1:8 For I do not wish you, brothers,
In ignorance to remain,
Concerning the tribulation
Which to us in Asia came.

We were burdened excessively
Beyond our power to bear,
So that even of life itself
We had begun to despair.

1:9 But we were brought to be convinced
Of the sentence of death's bed,
So we would not trust in ourselves
But God who raises the dead.

1:10 God spared us from such a great death
And will continue to spare.
We have hope in Him to do this
1:11 Because of your help in prayer.

Your prayer for us has resulted
In thanksgiving to the Lord
By many people for this gift
Through the many prayers implored.

1:12 For this is the boast that we have:
Our conscience testifies true
How we have been made to relate
In the world but more toward you.

We've acted with integrity,
With God-like sincerity,
Not in the wisdom of the flesh
But God's grace *and charity.

1:13 For we write you nothing except
What you read or comprehend.
I hope you will continue on
Understanding to the end.

1:14 As you have understood in part,
Your boast in us you must learn
Just like we will boast about you
The day of the Lord's return.

1:15 In this assurance that I have,
I was planning to come before
So that you might be doubly blessed
1:16 In me coming two times more.

Once in route to Macedonia,
And again returning from there,
Then to be helped into Judea
By you ◆through what you share.

1:17 Therefore, was I vacillating
When I planned this? There's no way![121]
Or was I planning in the flesh
So both yes and no I could say?

1:18 But as sure as God is faithful,
So too are the words we bestow,
Namely that what we speak to you
Is never both yes and no.

1:19 For Jesus Christ was preached by us
To you all as God's own Son.
That word was not both yes and no,
But in Him "yes" it's become.

Jesus Christ was preached by us three,
Silas, Timothy, and me,
1:20 For all the promises of God
In Christ, are a certainty.

Therefore, also through Jesus Christ
Is the Amen we proclaim
Unto God *for those promises
To the glory of His name.

1:21 God secures us with you in Christ.
Us He anointed and sealed.
1:22 He gave us the Spirit in our hearts
As a pledge *of what He's revealed.

1:23 Now I myself call upon God
As a witness to my soul:
I withdrew from coming to Corinth
To spare you *from my patrol.

1:24 Not that we are over your faith
To control it by demand,
But we're coworkers for your joy,
For by your own faith you stand.

2:1 For this I decided for myself
That I would not come again
Before you in a grievous state,
For who would benefit then?*

2:2 For if I myself cause you grief,
Then who would make me rejoice?
Would someone grieved because of me
Arise with a joyful voice?*

2:3 So, I wrote you the way I did[122]
So that when I do come back
I would obtain no grief from those
Whose joy toward me should not lack.

So, I wrote you the way I did,
Persuaded that you'd all act,
Because my joy is seeing you all
In a joyful state. *That's fact.

2:4 For out of much tribulation
And anguish within my heart,
I wrote to you through many tears
So from sin, you would depart.*

I did not write so you'd be grieved.
That's not what I wrote it for,◆
But so you'd realize that for you
My love abounds even more.

2:5 Now if someone has produced grief
(I speak with the greatest care),*
He has not alone caused me grief,
But in that grief you all share.

I speak like this* not to burden
With guilt's authority.*
2:6 Such one got ample punishment
By the majority.

2:7 So then, in contrast now forgive.
Give compassionate relief.
That way such one does not become
Swallowed up by excess grief.

2:8 Therefore, I urge that you confirm
Your love for such one this way.
2:9 Also I wrote so as to test
If in all things you obey.

2:10 Now whomever is forgiven,
I also forgive the same.
In fact, I have forgiven it.
The specifics I won't name.*

If I have forgiven something,
It's for you before Christ's face
2:11 So Satan won't handicap us.
His schemes we know to displace.

2:12 Now after coming to Troas
For the gospel of Christ's sake,
And walking through an opened door
Which the Lord to me did make -

2:13 I had no rest in my spirit,
With no signs of getting better
Since I could not find my brother,
Titus, who brought you my letter.[123]

But tearing myself from those there,
To Macedonia, I went.[124]
2:14 Thank God for always leading us
In triumph to Christ's extent.

Thank God for always revealing
Through us as His instrument
The aroma of His knowledge
In every place *we are sent.

2:15 For we are Christ's fragrance to God
Among all whose paths we've crossed,◆
Among those who are being saved,
And among those who are lost.[125]

2:16 To one a stench from death to death,
To another one there proceeds
A pleasing smell from life to life,
For who's ample for these deeds?

2:17 Unlike many who just peddle
The word of God as they've priced,
As from God in sincerity,
We speak in God's sight in Christ.

3:1 Must we commend ourselves again?
Or do we need, like some do,
A letter of commendation,
A letter to or from you?

3:2 You yourselves are our own letter
Which in our hearts was composed,
A letter well-known and read by all,
3:3 Not hidden, but exposed.◆

It's being shown that you're Christ's letter
Under our service and care,
Not written on tablets of stone
But on human hearts, *that's where.

But it's not written on those hearts
By black ink *with human hands
But by the living God's Spirit.
3:4 In this our confidence stands.

Such confidence that we possess
We hold before God through Christ,
3:5 Not that we're self-sufficient to say
That from us all has sufficed.

Our sufficiency is from God
3:6 Who has made us qualified
As servants of a covenant
That is new *as prophesied.

It's new and isn't of the letter,
For the written letter kills,
But it's of the Holy Spirit
Who, within us, life instills.

3:7 Now the ministry that brought death,
Written on tablets of stone,
Was introduced in glory
As the face of Moses shone.

Although the brightness of his face
Was fading throughout the days,
The sons of Israel still could not
In the face of Moses gaze.

3:8 Now if this ministry of death
Was in glory brought about,
The ministry of the Spirit
Is more glorious, no doubt.[126]

3:9 If there's glory in the ministry
That brought in condemnation,
How much more abounds in glory
That one of justification.

3:10 For even that which had glory,
Had no glory in this case
Due to the surpassing glory
Of the covenant of grace.*

3:11 For if what is passing away
Through the means of glory came,
How much more exists in glory
That which will always remain.

3:12 Therefore, we use great confidence
Due to this hope we embrace,
3:13 Not as Moses who kept wearing
A veil to cover his face.

For what purpose was the covering?*
So Israel's sons in no way
Could fix their gaze into the end
Of what was fading away.

3:14 But their thinking became hardened,
For up to the present day
When the old covenant is read,
Unlifted that veil does stay.

It stays because only in Christ
Is the veil taken away.
3:15 But when Moses is being read,
Their heart is veiled to this day.

3:16 But whenever a person turns
To the Lord *in faith that's real,
The veil that lies over the heart
Is removed. *It can't conceal.

3:17 Now the Lord *who removes the veil
Is the Spirit specifically,
And where the Lord, the Spirit is,
There's freedom. ◆There's liberty.

3:18 Now we *who have turned to the Lord
Possess an uncovered face,
Reflecting as in a mirror
The glory of the Lord *of grace.

We ourselves are being transformed
Into His image, *hear it,
Ever increasing in glory
As from the Lord, the Spirit.

4:1 So then, having this ministry
Where the gospel we impart,*
Even as we were shown mercy,
We are not losing heart.

4:2 But we renounced the hidden things
Where all shame is undeterred.
We don't live underhandedly.
We don't falsify God's word.

But by disclosure of the truth
We commend ourselves *without fraud
To the conscience of all who hear
Before the presence of God.

4:3 Now if our gospel has been veiled,
It is veiled *among one kind,
Among those who are perishing,
Among the spiritually blind.◆

4:4 The god of this evil era
Has blinded, removing sight
From the minds of unbelievers
So that they can't see the light.

The light is the gospel message
Of the glory Christ displayed
Who's the very image of God,
And that gospel we've conveyed.*

4:5 For we do not proclaim ourselves
But Jesus Christ as the Lord.
As for ourselves, we're your bond slaves.
With Jesus, we're in accord.

4:6 For God who said *in creation,
"From darkness let there be light,"
He has caused to shine in our hearts
Something gloriously bright.

It is the light of the knowledge,
The experience of grace,[127]
The experience of God's glory
In Jesus's very face.

4:7 We have this treasure of glory
In vessels of earthy sod
So that the greatness of its power
Will not be from us but God.

4:8 For we're pressured in every way.
However, we're never confined.
We're perplexed by the things we face,
But to give up we've not resigned.

4:9 We are being persecuted,
But God's presence is not void.[128]
We're often knocked down to the ground,
But we are never destroyed.

4:10 We take about Jesus's death
In this body *of servitude
In order that Jesus's life
In our body might be viewed.

4:11 For we who live, keep on facing
For Jesus's sake death's threat
In order that His life be viewed
In our flesh that's mortal yet.

4:12 Therefore in us death is working
Since we live in servitude,*
But life is working in you all
Since in us His life you viewed.*

4:13 We have the same spirit of faith
That accords with what's exclaimed
In the Scriptures by the psalmist,[129]
"I believed, so I proclaimed."

For we also keep believing
And so keep proclaiming too,
Having in the face of death's threat*
The resurrection in view.*

4:14 Because we know that He who raised
The Lord Jesus *will death undo,
So with Jesus, He will raise us,
Presenting us along with you.

4:15 For everything is for your sakes
So as grace abounds to more,
Many thanksgivings will abound.
God's glory it is all for.

4:16 Therefore, we are not losing heart,
Though the outer is in decay,
But not so with our inner man
Who's being renewed each day.

4:17 For our tribulation that's light
And merely transitory,
Produces for us so much more,
An endless weight of glory.

4:18 So we don't look at what is seen
Whose end will one day be due.
It's the unseen that's eternal.
Therefore, we keep that in view.

5:1 For we know that if ◆this body,
This earthly house where we dwell,
Becomes torn down, becomes destroyed,
There's a house that does excel.*

From God we have this other one,
A building that always stands,
An eternal house where we'll dwell,
Made in heaven without hands.

5:2 For we just groan *in this body,
Having an intense desire
To wear the clothes of our dwelling,
Our heavenly attire.

5:3 And when at last we wear those clothes,
We will not be found exposed,
5:4 For those in this earthly dwelling
Groan under burdens imposed.

For we don't want to be unclothed
But to be clothed, ◆that's the goal,
In order that what is mortal
Might by life be swallowed whole.

5:5 Now God is the one who prepared
For us this very event,
Giving to us the deposit
Of the Spirit *whom He sent.

5:6 Therefore, we're always confident,
Knowing this truth *as we roam
Although we're absent from the Lord
While in this body at home.

5:7 For we walk by faith, not by sight,
5:8 Preferring with bold accord
To be absent from our body
And to be home with the Lord.

5:9 So, whether at home or absent,
Whatever our condition,◆
To be well-pleasing to the Lord
Is our focused ambition.

5:10 For it is a necessity
For all of us to appear
Before the platform of Christ's throne
For the deeds we've done down here.

Each one will receive as he's done
In the body *of this earth,
Whether those deeds be something good
Or be something of no worth.

5:11 Therefore, knowing to fear the Lord,
We work at persuading mankind.
Just who we are, God clearly sees,
Which I hope your consciences find.

5:12 We are not commending again
Ourselves *by what we have said,
But a basis we're giving you
Of boasting for us instead.

This way you'll have something for those
Who opposition impart,*
Those who boast of appearances
Instead of what's in the heart.

5:13 If we were perceived as crazy,
Only God we had in view.
If we're condemned for sound thinking,
It is to benefit you.

5:14 For the love which Christ has for us
Compels us since we did decide
That one perished in place of all.
So in that One* all have died.

5:15 He died for all, so those who live
Would no more live to be praised,
But would live relating to Him
Who died for them and was raised.

5:16 From now on we know no one
By a fleshly view, therefore.
Though we've thus experienced Christ,
It's not that way anymore.

5:17 So, if anyone is in Christ,
That one is newly created.
Everything old is passed away.
The new has been activated.

5:18 All of these new things are from God
Who through Christ with us made peace.
A reconciling ministry
To us He did release.

5:19 God has placed in us this message
Of reconciliation,
Namely, that God has worked through Christ
To bring the world salvation.◆

He worked through Christ to reconcile
To Himself the world of men
By not counting their trespasses
At all against any of them.

5:20 So, we are Christ's ambassadors,
God's urgings through us compiled.
We beg you, on behalf of Christ,
To God become reconciled.

5:21 For He who did not ever sin
Was made sin for us, *the flawed,
So that we might become in Christ
The righteousness of God.

6:1 Now as those who labor with God,
We too urge you to refrain
From receiving the grace of God
In a manner that is vain.

6:2 For He says, "At the welcomed time
Attention to you I paid,
And in the day of salvation
I came to give you My aid."

Therefore, take very careful note
That now is the welcomed time.
Also, take very careful note
That salvation's day is prime.

6:3 We do not give an occasion
For any to trip ◆or fall
So that the ministry of God
Might not be faulted at all.

6:4 But in all things we do commend
Ourselves as servants of God,
Enduring much adversity
As we travel abroad.*

We endure in tribulations,
In hardships and distresses,
6:5 In beatings, in imprisonments,
And in riots that oppress us.

We endure through many labors,
Often lacking sleep ◆and rest,
And at times we serve in hunger,
Having nothing to digest.*

6:6 But we serve God in purity,
In a patience of great length,
In both knowledge and in kindness,
In the Holy Spirit's *strength.

And in genuine love we serve.
6:7 With the word of truth we fight
In God's power through righteous weapons
For the left hand and the right.

6:8 Yet it is paradoxical*
How others might us receive:*
With glory yet with dishonor,
As true yet as those who deceive.

Some will give us a good report.
Others slander our mission.
6:9 Although we are very well-known,
Some give no recognition.

Some see us as those bound to die,
Yet behold we still have breath!
We're viewed as those who are punished,
Yet we are not put to death.

6:10 Though we're grieved, we ever rejoice.
Though poor, with riches we bless.
Though we have nothing *on this earth,
All things we really possess.

6:11 O Corinthians, we've opened up,
There's nothing that we did hide.*
Our mouth has openly spoken,
And our heart has opened wide.

6:12 You are not restricted by us
But by your own affections.
6:13 You're like my children. So respond.
Open up *without objections.

6:14 Do not be unequally yoked
With unbelievers, ever.
Can righteousness and lawlessness
Truly be partners? *Never!

Or what fellowship can exist
Between what's light and what's dark?
6:15 Or between Christ and the Devil[130]
Can harmony make its mark?

Believers and unbelievers,
What is common in their case?
6:16 What agreement is there between
Idols and God's dwelling place?

We ourselves are the dwelling place
Of the God who is living.
Just as God said *in the Scriptures,
Which quotes I'll now be giving:*

"I will dwell and walk among them,
And their God I will become,
And they will be My own people.
6:17 Therefore, *I call to each one:

"'Separate! Come out from their midst'
(The Lord says *to those who believe),
'And stop touching what is unclean,
And you all I will receive.

6:18 "'And a father to you I'll be,
And by Me, you'll be adored.*
You'll be My sons and My daughters,'
Says the Almighty Lord."

7:1 Therefore, having these promises,
Let us all our own selves cleanse
From all defilement of the flesh
And of the spirit, my friends.

At the same time that we do this,
Let us all work to perfect
Our individual holiness
As God, we fear ◆and respect.

7:2 Make room for us *in your own hearts.
To wrong no one we've managed.
There is no one we've corrupted.
Not one we've disadvantaged.

7:3 I do not say this to condemn,
For you these words I did give,
You're in our hearts so that with you
We've died to sin[131] and now live.

7:4 My faith and pride in you is great.
Your comfort has filled me up.
In all of our tribulation
My joy overflows *its cup.

7:5 For even to Macedonia
We came with no bodily rest.
Conflicts without and fears within,
On every side, we were pressed.

7:6 However, God, who gives comfort
To those who are downhearted,
Comforted us when Titus came
After from you he parted.*

7:7 But not only in his coming
Were we by comfort relieved,
But in the encouragement too
That he from you had received.

He informed us of your longing
And of your lamentation,
And also of your zeal for me.
So, I had more elation.

7:8 For even though I caused you grief
In the letter which I wrote,
I do not have any regrets,
Though this regret I did note.

I felt regret after I saw
How the letter caused you grief.
However, this painful status
Was for a time that was brief.

7:9 So, presently I'm rejoicing,
Not because you all were grieved,
But because of your repentance
That in time your grief achieved.

It was God's will that you were grieved
For the time which we did note◆
So you'd suffer no loss from us
By anything which we wrote.

7:10 For godly grief works repentance
To salvation without regrets,
But a grief that is from the world,
Death is what it begets.

7:11 Look at how great an earnestness
This very grief we induced,
Which was according to God's will,
Has within you been produced:

Such defensive speech for your case,
For sin* such indignation,
Such fear, such great desire, such zeal,
Of wrong such vindication.

In everything that you had done,
Yourselves you all did commend
To be innocent in the case
Of the one who did offend.[132]

7:12 Therefore, although I wrote you all,
It was not for that one's sake
Or for that of the offended,
But your earnestness to awake.

I wrote you all on this matter
In order that you'd realize
The earnestness you have for us
Before God's very eyes.

7:13 So, by this we've been comforted,
And besides, we're much more blessed
As we exulted with Titus
Since his spirit, you refreshed.

7:14 Because if there is anything
I've boasted to him of you,
I was not put to shame by it.
My boast was found to be true.

For even as we spoke in truth
About everything to you,
So our boasting we told Titus
Was also found to be true.

7:15 His affection for you increased
As he recalls how you obeyed,
How you welcomed him when he came,
With fear and trembling displayed.

7:16 So, I'm currently rejoicing.
My joy for you is immense*
Because in every single thing
In you I have confidence.

8:1 Now we acquaint you all, brothers,
With God's grace that's been gifted
By the Macedonian churches,
8:2 Although greatly afflicted.

That the abundance of their joy
And of their deep poverty
Overflowed into the riches
Of their generosity.

8:3 That by their own ability,
Even beyond it, I attest,
They all gave of their own choosing.
By no one were they pressed.*

8:4 They were actually begging us
That they could, *without restraints,
Participate in the giving,
In the ministry to the saints.

8:5 And we did not expect from them
How all this they would fulfill.
First, they gave themselves to the Lord
And then to us by God's will.

8:6 So then, Titus we encouraged
That, as with you he did start,
In the same way, he would complete
This gracious gift on your part.

8:7 Just as in all things you abound,
In faith, in knowledge, in speech,
In all diligence, and in love
Inspired by us *who preach -

Just as in all things you abound,
And in nothing have you lacked,*
We also urge you to abound
In this gift, this gracious act.

8:8 I'm not giving you a command,
But I'm approving, *brothers,
The genuineness of your love
Through the diligence of others.

8:9 For you're acquainted with the grace
Of our Lord Jesus Christ,
That although He was very rich,
For your sakes *He sacrificed.

He became poor on your account
So that in His poverty
You might become completely filled
With His prosperity.

8:10 My advice: giving profits you.
You were not just first to start,
But a year ago desired first
In this service to take part.*

8:11 And now complete this gracious act
In the same eagerness shown.
Be as eager to fulfill it
By giving from what you own.

8:12 For if the readiness to give
Is set before your own eyes,
It's accepted by what you have
Not by your lack of supplies.

8:13 For this is not so that others
Might rest *in frivolity
While you sink in tribulation,
But it's for equality.

8:14 As of this time your abundance
Is for others who now lack
So that when they have abundance,
Your need can be supplied back.

That way there is equality,
8:15 Just as in Scripture we read:[133]
"He who had much, had no excess.
He who had less, had no need."

8:16 But praise and* blessings unto God
Who placed in Titus's heart
The same diligence for you all
That to you we do impart.*

8:17 Because, you see, on the one hand
He gave into our urging,
But yet he came to you freely
With more diligence emerging.

8:18 We've sent with him that one brother
Who's been the object of praise
For his service to the gospel
By all the churches *these days.

8:19 And not just this, but he as well
By the churches was selected
To travel in our company
As we carry what's collected.

This grace that we administer
Serves these reasons *you must know:
So as to glorify the Lord
And our readiness to show.

8:20 We want to dodge criticism,
Bearing a gift of great size,
8:21 For in the sight of God and men
We respect what's good and wise.

8:22 Now we've sent with them our brother
Whom we have often tested
In relation to many things,
And this was manifested:

He demonstrated diligence,
But as to his present state,
He's more diligent since in you
His confidence is so great.

8:23 If someone asks about Titus,
Inform with this point of view:*
He's my partner and coworker
In relationship to you.

And as for our other brothers,
If asked, let this be sufficed:
They are sent out[134] from the churches
And are a glory to Christ.

8:24 Therefore, to them please demonstrate
Before all the churches' sight
The proof of your unselfish love
And our boast of you as right.

9:1 For concerning the ministry
To the saints *who are in need,
To keep writing to you of this
Is superfluous indeed.

9:2 For I know you're ready to give,
And of this, I have taken pride,
Telling the Macedonians
What Achaians did decide.

I informed them that since last year
You've already been prepared,
And your zeal stirred up more of them.
So, in this giving they shared.*

9:3 But I have sent brothers to you
So our pride would not prove vain,
So you'd become fully prepared
As before I did explain.

9:4 Or else, if Macedonians
Were to accompany me
And find you all unprepared,
What would the effect then be?*

We certainly would be ashamed
(Not to mention, so would you)
In this confidence of ours
That there would be follow through.*

9:5 Therefore, I thought that the brothers
Just had to be entreated
To come to you ahead of us
For what you've not completed.[135]

They are coming to prearrange
The blessing[136] *you wish to share
Which you had promised beforehand.
A year ago you did swear.[137]

They're doing this so the blessing
Might be properly prepared,
Not reflecting covetousness
But a gift generously shared.

9:6 Now listen *to this principle
From a proverb that we read.[138]
The harvest reaped from what is sown*
Depends on the amount of seed.*

He who sows very little seed,
A small harvest he will reap,
But he who sows many blessings,
Many blessings on him will heap.

9:7 As each one resolves in his heart,
That promise he must deliver,*
Not out of sorrow nor duress,
For God loves a cheerful giver.

9:8 God can increase all grace to you
So that you, having all you need
All the time and in everything,
Might abound for every good deed.

9:9 This agrees with what's been written,
"He scattered, sowing much seed.
His righteousness always remains.
He gave to those who had need."

9:10 And He who supplies all the seed
To the sower to be sown,
And He who supplies bread for food
From the seed that has been thrown -

He will provide your seed to sow,
And it, He will multiply,
And He'll increase your righteousness.
This harvest He will supply.

9:11 In everything you'll be enriched
So you can generously share,
Which brings forth thanksgiving to God
Through us *as your gifts we bear.

9:12 For this ministry of service
Is not just meeting the saints' needs,
But also thanksgivings to God
Abound *in these multiplied seeds.

9:13 Since this ministry is approved,
Glory to God these saints give
Based upon your choice to submit
And how you've chosen to live.*

You're living out your confession
In the gospel of the Christ
As among them and among all
You share what you sacrificed.

9:14 They yearn for you in their prayers
Since God's great grace on you is poured.
9:15 For His indescribable gift,
God is blessed *and adored!

10:1 I, Paul, who am meek when present
But bold with words when away,
Through Christ's gentle and kind nature
I exhort you *to obey.

10:2 I am begging you *to obey
So that when I am present,
I won't be bold with confidence,
Which would be most unpleasant.*

For I'm thinking about coming
Against some with my bold talk
Who say according to the flesh
That we continually walk.

10:3 For although we're walking in flesh
(This body that all observe),*
It's not according to the flesh
That we as God's soldiers serve.[139]

10:4 For the weapons of our warfare
Aren't fleshly, but hold God's might
For the destruction of strongholds,
Tearing down *what is not right.

We tear down human reasonings
10:5 And all loftiness raised high
That's against the knowledge of God
By the weapons we apply.*

Yes, we're taking as prisoners
In this spiritual crusade*
Each and every single thought
So that Christ might be obeyed.

10:6 And every disobedience
We are ready to chastise
Whenever your obedience
You fulfill ◆and finalize.

10:7 Keep looking at the obvious.
If someone is confident
That he truly belongs to Christ,
Let him think to this extent:*

Let that person reconsider
How of Christ he came to be,
And realize that as he's of Christ,
So also of Christ are we.

10:8 For as to our authority,
If my boasting that I've claimed
Seems to be somewhat excessive,
I will not be ashamed.

For this very authority,
Which to us the Lord bestowed,
Is to build up, not destroy,
And to you, that's what we showed.

10:9 I say all this in order that
To you, I may not appear
As one attempting through letters
To produce in you great fear.

10:10 For someone says, *and this I quote,
"His letters have weight and clout,
But his speech is unimpressive.
Strength of presence he's without."

10:11 But let such one consider this:
When we are away and write,
Such as we are in word, we'll be
In action when in full sight.

10:12 For we're not bold to classify
Or compare ourselves with some
Who work at commending themselves,
For unwise these have become.

They are not wise because of this:
They all measure and compare
Just who they are among themselves.
But in this standard they err.*

10:13 We will not boast beyond measure
But according to one *that's true,
The standard God apportioned us,
Which reaches working with you.

10:14 For we're not above our limits
As though you, we should not reach,
For we were first to come to you
With the gospel of Christ *and preach.

10:15 We're not boasting beyond measure,
That is, in the work of others,
But we hope our work is enlarged
Even beyond you, *my brothers.

As your faith grows among you all,
We hope our work does expand
According to the same standard
Apportioned us by God's hand.[140]

10:16 To preach the gospel is our hope
Beyond your town's location,
Not boasting in another's work
From the Lord's preparation.

10:17 Let the one who keeps on boasting
Place pride in the Lord alone,
10:18 For the one who commends himself
Has a standard of his own.*

That one is not approved at all.
He has not passed any test.*
But the one whom the Lord commends,
Approval he has possessed.

11:1 Oh that you would put up with me
As in foolishness, I dabble,
But of course you'll put up with me
In a little foolish babble.

11:2 For I am jealous over you
With the jealousy of God.
I joined you to one husband, Christ,
As a virgin who's unflawed.

11:3 But I'm afraid that as with Eve
The serpent slyly enticed,
Somehow your minds might be spoiled
From focused purity in Christ.

11:4 For if one comes preaching Jesus
As another, *which you can tell,
And not as He whom we have preached,
You still put up with it well.

Or you get a different Spirit
Whom you did not from us receive,
Or you get a different gospel
In which you did not believe.[141]

11:5 For I do not think of myself
To be one who's inferior
To the ones who proclaim to be
Apostolically superior.

11:6 Yet even if unskilled in speech,
In knowledge, I'm not that way,
But both in all and among all
This knowledge to you we display.

11:7 Was it sin to humble myself?
Am I one to be faulted*
Since I preached God's gospel for free
So you might be exalted?

11:8 In fact,* I robbed other churches
By receiving compensation
For the purpose of serving you
So you'd have no obligation.*

11:9 Even when I was there with you
And came to be in great need,
I didn't burden any of you,
For others did a great deed.*

The Macedonian brothers
Came and my need supplied.
Each case I did not burden you,
And I will not. That's my pride.

11:10 As the truth of Christ is in me,
This pride of mine won't be stopped
In the regions of Achaia
Where to charge I did not opt.[142]

11:11 For what reason did I choose this?
What reason do you suppose*
That selfless love for you I lack?
My selfless love* God knows.

11:12 But I'll keep doing what I do
To cut off all occasion
From those who desire to be found
Like us in their self-inflation.

11:13 For such ones are false apostles.
They are workers that mislead.
They masquerade as Christ's apostles.
11:14 No wonder they do this deed.

For as a messenger of light,
Satan does himself disguise.
11:15 Therefore, if his servants deceive,
It is of no great surprise.

They disguise themselves as servants
Of righteousness, *as they say,
But corresponding to their works
Their end will arrive one day.

11:16 I repeat, let none deem me foolish,
Or else if a fool I befit,
Receive me, *as you have others,
So I can boast a wee bit.

11:17 What I say in this bold boasting
I don't speak as the Lord would,
But speak as one in foolishness,
Not in a way that I should.*

11:18 Since many boast in their own flesh,
This I'll also duplicate.
11:19 For you think you are wise, yet fools
You gladly tolerate.

11:20 If one enslaves you, you endure.
If you, someone devours
Or in some way takes advantage,
You let them exert their powers.*

If above you one lifts himself,
Or if someone slaps your face,
In whatever these fools have done,*
Toleration you embrace.

11:21 I speak with no honor when I say
That we have been very weak.
In whatever things someone boasts,
In foolish boldness, I'll speak.

11:22 Are they Hebrews? Well, I am too.
Are they Israelites? So am I.
Are they Abraham's descendants?
To me, this too does apply.

11:23 Are they servants of Jesus Christ?
I speak as if I'm insane.
I'm even more of a servant.
So, let me briefly explain.*

In far more labors I have served,
In much more imprisonments,
In beatings that are more severe,
And often in death's suspense.

11:24 Five times I received from the Jews
Thirty-nine stripes *on the back;
11:25 Three times I was beaten with rods;
Once stoned *in a mob's attack.[143]

In three distinct situations
I abandoned a shipwrecked boat;
An entire day and one whole night
In the deep, I spent afloat.

11:26 In more frequent journeys I've served,
Facing dangers all the miles,*
Dangers of rivers and robbers,
Dangers from Jews and Gentiles.

I've faced dangers in the city,
Dangers in the desert trail,
Dangers among so-called brothers,
Dangers in the sea we sail.

11:27 In labor and in toil I've served,
Often going without sleep,
In the cold and in exposure,
Without clothes my warmth to keep.*

I've served in hunger and in thirst,
Often with no food to digest.
11:28 Besides, with care for all the churches
Every day I am hard-pressed.

11:29 Who's weak without me being weak?
Or who is caused to stumble
Without me being set on fire
Against him who caused the tumble?*

11:30 If it's essential that I boast,
I will boast about these things
Having to do with my weakness,
For glory to God this brings.*

11:31 The Father of our Lord Jesus Christ,
Who's God eternally blessed,
He knows that I am not lying
About these things I've expressed.*

11:32 In Damascus, the governor,
Under Aretas the king,
Set his guards at the city gates
So upon me, he could spring.

11:33 And through a window in the wall,
In a basket I was let down,
Able to escape from his hands
As I went away from that town.*

12:1 It's now necessary to boast,
And though there's no reward,[144]
I will now move on to visions
And revelations from the Lord.

12:2 I know about a man in Christ,
Over fourteen years ago,
Who was snatched to the third heaven.
In what way I do not know.

Whether he was in his body
As into this heaven, he rose,*
Or if he was outside of it,
I'm ignorant, but God knows.

12:3 And I know about such a man
Who was snatched to Paradise.
If bodily or not, who knows?
God knows, *and that does suffice.

12:4 He heard inexpressible words,
Not allowed for a man to speak.
12:5 About such a man I will boast.
As for myself, just of what's weak.

12:6 For if I really wished to boast
About this revelation*
I would not be a fool and lie.
Truth would be my oration.

But I'll refrain from speaking this
So that me no one will deem
Above that which he hears me preach
Or what in me he has seen.

12:7 Because of the excessiveness
Of the revelations made,
So I might not exalt myself,
Mistreatment on me was laid.

I was given a thorn in the flesh,[145]
A messenger of Satan
To oppose me and mistreat me,
To prevent self-exaltation.

12:8 Concerning this thorn in the flesh,
Three times I begged the Lord
That He take it away from me.
My three prayers were not ignored.*

12:9 He said to me, "My gift of grace
For you, it is all you need,
For in weakness power is made
To attain its goal, indeed."

Therefore, gladly I'll rather boast
In weaknesses for me meant
In order that the power of Christ
Might upon me pitch its tent.[146]

12:10 So, in weaknesses I'm content,
In hardships, in insults of wrong,
In tough[147] persecutions for Christ.
For when I am weak, I'm strong.

12:11 I've become foolish in this talk,
Which you compelled me to do,
For I should have been commended
Not by myself, but by you.

For though I myself am nothing,
I still am not inferior
To those who think themselves to be
Apostolically superior.

12:12 The signs of a true apostle
Among you were introduced.
Signs and wonders and miracles
In all patience were produced.

12:13 For compared to other churches,
Were you treated worse all along?
I only did not burden you.
Forgive me if this was wrong.

12:14 Look, I'm ready to come to you,
And this will be the third time,
And I still will not burden you.
I will not charge you a dime.*

For I don't seek the things you have,
That is, the treasures you own,*
But I only am seeking you,
Yes, just you, and you alone.*

To store treasures for their parents,
Children are not mandated,
But to store up for their children,
Parents are obligated.

12:15 And I myself will gladly spend,
Even be spent for your lives.
Or will you love me any less
If my love for you just thrives?

12:16 Granted, I did not burden you.
But did you, I wrongly treat
By cunningly *not charging you
To capture you by deceit?

12:17 Did I take advantage of you
Through any I sent your way?[148]
12:18 I urged Titus with the brother
To you a visit pay.

Titus took no advantage of you.[149]
This you would have to confess.*
Didn't we walk in the same spirit,
In the same footsteps? Yes![150]

12:19 In this you're thinking that to you
Our own selves we are defending.
But in Christ, we speak these words
Which before God are ascending.

All these things that we write, my friends,
Are for your edification.
12:20 For in my coming to see you,
I have fear ◆and trepidation.

I fear that I might find you all
In a state I don't want to see,
And also, that I might be found
Not like you wish me to be.

I might find strife and jealousy,
Wrath and selfish ambition,
Slander, gossip, and arrogance,
And chaotic exhibition.

12:21 Again, I fear that when I come,
You might see me as I did warn.
God might humble me before you,
And over many, I might mourn -

Mourn over those who've sinned before,
Yet repentance they did forbid
Of the uncleanness and lewdness
And immorality they did.

13:1 I'm coming to you a third time.
This Scripture we have applied:*
"By two or three witnesses
Every case must be ratified."

13:2 As I mentioned previously
When with you the second time,
And now while far away from you,
I give this warning of mine.

I forewarn you who've sinned before
And everyone else as well,
That when I come to you again,
I won't spare *those who rebel.

13:3 For you're seeking proof of the Christ
As One who in me does speak.
Full of power He deals with you.
Toward you, He is not weak.

13:4 For even though out of weakness
He was nailed to the cross *He bore,
Now out of the power of God
He lives on *forevermore.

For we ourselves, since we're in Him,
To the world* we're also weak,
But by the power of God toward you
We'll live with Him as we speak.

13:5 Keep on testing yourselves to see
If in the faith you reside.
Keep on examining yourselves
To see if Christ lives inside.

Or have you not about yourselves
Come to realize *what you've professed,
That Christ is living within you?
Unless you have failed the test.

13:6 But I hope that you will realize
That we have not failed the test.
13:7 And I keep on praying to God
That in wrong you won't invest.

I don't pray this to prove ourselves
As seeming to pass the test,
But so you might practice what's good
Though as failures we're assessed.

13:8 For we're able to do nothing
Against the truth *and prevail.
Only on behalf of the truth
Can we act *and not fail.

13:9 For we rejoice when we are weak
While power on you is poured.
And this also we are praying,
For you all to be restored.

13:10 Because of this I write these things
While far away *and not near
So that, when I'm in your presence,
I won't have to be severe.

I act by the authority
Which to me the Lord supplied
In order that edification,
Not destruction be applied.

13:11 As I close this letter, brothers,
I am bidding you farewell.[151]
Keep yourselves in superb repair.
Encouragement don't repel.

Focus your mind on the same thing.
Peace among you be your call.
This way the God of love and peace
Will surely be with you all.

13:12 A kiss described as set apart,[152]
To one another extend.
13:13 All the saints *that are here with me,
Greetings to you they send.

13:14 The grace of the Lord Jesus Christ,
And God's love *that does enthrall,
And the Holy Spirit's fellowship,
Are certainly with you all![153]

THE POETIC LETTER TO THE GALATIANS

1:1 I, Paul, who am an apostle
(Not by means of the design
Of any man or group of men
But through Him who is divine - [154]

Through Jesus Christ and Father God
Who raised Him from death *by might),
1:2 I and all the brothers with me
To the Galatian churches *write.

1:3 To all of you *I write these words:
Grace and peace on you are poured,[155]
Which proceed from God our Father
And from Jesus Christ the Lord.

1:4 Who in substitute for our sins
Himself He did freely give
To save us from this evil age
In which we presently live.

'Twas from our God and Father's will
That His sacrifice did stem.
1:5 All the glory and praise to God
Forevermore! Amen.

1:6 I am shocked that you so quickly
From God are turning away,
Him who called you in connection
With the grace of Christ *that day.

I'm shocked that another gospel
You are just running toward,
1:7 Which is not even similar
To the gospel of our Lord.

There are some who are troubling you,
Desiring to modify
The gospel about Jesus Christ,
And so making it a lie.*

1:8 If we were to preach a gospel
Besides the one preached at first,
Or an angel from heaven did,
Let that preacher be accursed.

1:9 What we have said, I state again,
Let that preacher be accursed
Who preaches to you a gospel
Besides what you received at first.

1:10 For am I now trying to gain
Approval from men or God?
Or do I continually work
So that me, men would applaud?

If I were trying to please men,
Then I would no longer be
A bond slave of Jesus the Christ
Who gave the gospel to me.*

1:11 For I, brothers, make known to you
That the gospel I proclaim
Did not come from any human,
But by revelation came.◆

1:12 For I received it not from man,
Nor by a man was I taught.
Through a revelation by Christ[156]
This gospel to me was brought.◆

1:13 For you have heard of my past life,
Entrenched in the Jewish ways,
When I tried to destroy God's church,
Persecuting greatly *those days.

1:14 I was advancing far beyond
Many of those from my nation
Who were my contemporaries
In religious education.[157]

For my zeal was overflowing
For the Jewish traditions
Handed down from my ancestors,
Fueling my ambitions.*

1:15 But when God was pleased to reveal
His own Son in my case,
Who chose me from my mother's womb
And who called me by His grace –

1:16 When God did this so I'd preach Christ
Among Gentiles as good news,
To get advice from flesh and blood
I did not right away choose.

1:17 I didn't go to Jerusalem
To Christ's apostolic pack,[158]
But I went into Arabia,
Then to Damascus came back.

1:18 Three years later, *after God's call,[159]
Into Jerusalem, I went
To get acquainted with Cephas.
Fifteen days with him I spent.

1:19 As for the remaining apostles,
I didn't see any other,
Except I saw just one of them.
I saw James, the Lord's brother.[160]

1:20 (Before God I am not lying.
Accept this writing I've sent.)*
1:21 Into the regions of Syria
And Cilicia I then went.

1:22 Yet by churches[161] in Judea,
The ones gathered in Christ's name,
I was not recognized by face.
Just my actions were my fame.*

1:23 For about me they heard just this:
"He who used to persecute
Us *who believed in Jesus Christ
Is now in a different pursuit.*

"Now he's preaching the news of faith
Which he once tried to destroy."
1:24 And so, you see, because of me,
They were praising God with joy.

2:1 I went again to Jerusalem
During a fourteen year span,[162]
Barnabas and Titus with me,
In accordance to ◆God's plan.

2:2 Yes, I went in accordance to
A revelation that came,
And laid before them the gospel
That to Gentiles I proclaim.

But 'twas in private before them
Who others' respect did gain
So they could see whether or not
I might or had run in vain.

2:3 But Titus who was there with me,
Though obviously a Greek,
Wasn't compelled to be circumcised
Because of those who did sneak.

2:4 For false brothers sneaked to spy out
The freedom to us *God gave,
The kind we have in Jesus Christ.
Us they wanted to enslave.

2:5 But to them we did not yield
In subjection for one second[163]
In order that before your eyes
The gospel truth would stay reckoned.

2:6 But, by those who had gained respect,
On me was laid no restriction.
(Who they were, does not affect me.
God favors no man's position.)

2:7 But they saw that just as Peter
Had been called by God to the Jews,[164]
So I for the uncircumcised
Had been entrusted the good news.

2:8 For He who worked apostleship
In Peter to the circumcised,
Also in me to the Gentiles
Apostleship authorized.

2:9 Since they saw this grace given me,
James, Cephas, and John, *these three,
Gave their right hands of fellowship
To both Barnabas and me.

Those three who are viewed as pillars,
In this action strategized
That we go preach to the Gentiles
And they to the circumcised.

2:10 Just this one thing did they insist:
To keep mindful of the poor,
The very thing in eagerness
That I had done before.

2:11 When Cephas came to Antioch,
A situation arose.*
Because he had condemned himself,
To his face, I did oppose.

2:12 You see, before certain people
Had come from James *to correct,
Eating his meals with the Gentiles,
Peter did always elect.

But when they came, Peter began
To withdraw and separate
Since those of the circumcision
He feared *with a fear so great.

2:13 And the rest of the Jews joined him
In hypocrisy that day.
Barnabas too in this pretense
Was being carried away.

2:14 But when I saw that their actions
Didn't match the gospel of grace,[165]
In the presence of everyone
I told Cephas to his face:[166]

"If you, although being a Jew,
Live as if a Gentile would,
Why keep urging that like a Jew
To live the Gentiles should?

2:15 "We're not sinners from among Gentiles.
We're Jews by means of our birth,
2:16 But we came to know how a man
Gains righteousness of true worth.*

"By the works that derive from law[167]
A man is not justified.[168]
Only through faith in Jesus Christ
Can righteousness be applied.*

"And we ourselves for this purpose
In Jesus Christ came to believe:
In order that by faith in Christ
Righteousness we might receive.

"So by one's legalistic works
Righteousness is not applied,
Since by the works derived from law
No flesh will be justified.

2:17 "But let's assume that we ourselves
Are found as sinners *by some
While we're seeking to be declared
Righteous in Christ, *God's Son.

"Is Christ then a servant to sin?
That can't be true[169] *as you know.
2:18 For if I rebuild what I've torn down,[170]
As a sinner myself I show.

2:19 "For 'twas through law that I myself
To that law spiritually died
For the purpose that I might live,
Live to God *with faith applied.

2:20 "With Christ I have been crucified.
So, I'm no longer alive.
Christ is the One who lives in me.
So in Christ, I now survive.*

"The life I now live in this flesh
I live by faith in God's Son
Who loved me and gave Himself up
For me, *the undeserved one.

2:21 "God's grace I'm not nullifying,
For if righteousness is through law,
Then Christ died unnecessarily,
A wrong conclusion to draw."*

3:1 Oh Galatians! You are foolish!
Who is your bewitching guide?
Jesus was publicly portrayed
In your eyes as crucified.

3:2 I wish to learn from you one thing:
Did you receive the Spirit
By works of law or a word of faith?
Tell me. I wish to hear it.*

3:3 After starting in the Spirit,
Are you so foolish to try
To presently perfect yourselves,
In your own flesh to rely?

3:4 Have you suffered so many things
Without reason *in Christ's name?
(I am making the assumption
That it really was in vain.)

3:5 Therefore, *think about this question:
Why to you did God supply
His Spirit and His miracles?
You tell me the reason why.*

Was it because of works you did
Derived from a law you heard,
Or was it because you received
The message of faith, *God's word?

3:6 For this is just like Abraham
When righteousness he received.*
Faith was counted as righteousness
As soon as in God he believed.

3:7 So then, you personally know[171]
How Abraham's son one becomes.
People characterized by faith,
Only these are Abraham's sons.

3:8 And the Scripture clearly foresaw
That Gentiles are also the blessed.
God declared them righteous by faith,
The same faith Abraham possessed.*

For it's written in the Scripture
This promise that God expressed*
To Abraham well in advance,
"In you, all nations will be blessed."

3:9 So, those who are described by faith,
In accordance with God's plan*
Are being blessed right along with
The believer, Abraham.

3:10 For all those whose lives are described
By works that law does command
Are under a terrible curse.
Yes, under a curse they stand.◆

For it's written, "Each one is cursed
Who does not keep abiding
In all that's written in the Book,
The Book of the Law, ◆that writing."

3:11 It's clear that in the realm of law
No man with God is made right,
For "The righteous by faith will live"
Is the Scripture I must recite.[172]

3:12 The Law is not derived from faith.
This truth the Scripture does give:[173]
"All the ones who practice these things,
In these things must also live."

3:13 Christ redeemed us from the Law's curse,
Becoming in our place a curse.
For "He's cursed who hangs on a tree"
Is written *this Scripture verse.

3:14 This was so that to the Gentiles
The blessing of Abraham
Might be given in Christ Jesus.
This was God's eternal plan.*

This was so that each one of us
The promise would receive,
The promise of the Holy Spirit
Through faith, ◆when we believe.

3:15 Brothers, here's an illustration:
Once a covenant is okayed,
No one voids it or adds to it
Even though it is manmade.

3:16 But to Abraham and his seed
The promises God did state.
Now He did not say "and to seeds"
Which is a number that's great.*

But God promised "and to your seed."
Just one seed *was His intent,
Referring to just one person.
Christ is the seed that was meant.

3:17 Now this is what I am saying:
The promise was not negated
Four hundred thirty years later
When law became activated.

The implementation of law
Did not void what God ratified,
The covenant He previously made,
For the promise to set aside.

3:18 For assuming by means of law
The inheritance is gained,
Then it by means of a promise
No longer can be obtained.

But God has given Abraham
A gift that is undeserved
By means of a promise He made,
The inheritance reserved.*

3:19 Therefore then, what is the Law for?
'Twas added for sins, *understand,
Having been ordained through angels
In a mediator's hand.

The Law was added 'til the time
Of the coming of the seed,
To whom the promise had been made
Which in the Scripture we read.*

3:20 No mediator belongs to one.
For many he does intercede.*
But God, He is just one person.
No mediator does He need.*

3:21 Therefore, does the Law contradict
The promises *that God gave?
There is no way this can happen!
How then could God save?*

If a body of law was given
Which could produce life indeed,
Righteousness would have been by law.
No promises would we need.*

3:22 However, Scripture has confined
Under sin all *as unjust
So the promise by faith in Christ[174]
Might be given to those who trust.

3:23 But before that faith had arrived,
Under law we were protected,
Being confined for the faith
About to be shown *and effected.

3:24 Therefore, the Law in regards to Christ,
Our tutor, it had become
So we would be declared righteous
By faith *in Jesus, God's Son.

3:25 Now since that faith in Christ has come,
We're under a tutor no more.
3:26 Through your faith in Jesus the Christ,
You all are God's sons, therefore.

3:27 All you who were baptized into Christ
Have put on Christ, *so to speak.
Therefore, we conclude that* in Christ
3:28 There is neither Jew nor Greek.

There is neither slave nor freeman.
There's neither male nor female.
You are all one in Christ Jesus,
No distinction to prevail.◆

3:29 And because you belong to Christ,
Then you are Abraham's seed,
Heirs according to the promise
Which God to him guaranteed.*

4:1 I say, if an heir is a child,
Until he becomes mature,
He does not differ from a slave
Though all things he owns for sure.

4:2 But he is under guardians
And under stewards, 'til when?
Until the time his father set,
And not earlier than then.*

4:3 Similarly, while just children,
We too had been firmly bound
Under the basic principles
Of the world that does surround.

4:4 But when the fullness of time came,
God sent down His only Son.
From a woman and under law[175]
His earthly life[176] had begun.

4:5 He came this way in order to
Redeem all those under law
With the result that we'd receive
The adoption by Abba.

4:6 The word Abba just means Father.
And since you are sons to Him,
God sent His Son's Spirit to our hearts
Crying "Abba" from within.

4:7 So then, you are truly a son,
And a slave you are no more,
And if a son, an heir through God.
But look at what was before:*

4:8 When you had no knowledge of God,
Remember how you behaved.*
To those which by nature aren't gods
You all were truly enslaved.

4:9 But after coming to know God,
Personally I mean to say,[177]
Or rather after you became
Known by God in this way -

How then can you turn back again
Toward what's miserable and weak?
Bondage to worldly principles,
Why again do you wish to seek?

4:10 You closely observe days and months.
The seasons and years - the same.
4:11 I fear for you that possibly
I've labored for you in vain.

4:12 Become like me, for I'm like you.
Brothers, I beg; •I implore.
You did not mistreat me at all
When I preached to you before.*

4:13 I first preached the gospel to you
In sickness, as you well know,
4:14 And in my sickness was your trial
To receive me or forgo.*

You did not despise nor reject,
But instead, you welcomed me
As you would an angel of God,
Or Christ Jesus, *heartily.

4:15 Therefore, where is your happiness?
For to you, I testify:
If you could, by gouging yours out,
You'd have given me each eye.

4:16 So, by speaking the truth to you
Have I then become your foe?
4:17 Those false teachers[178] have zeal for you,
But it's not for good. *I know.

They wish to shut you out from me
So that for them you'd have zeal.
4:18 Now to always be zealous in good
Is surely a good ideal.

My children, not just when I'm there,
But with good zeal always *be draped.
4:19 For you I suffer birth pains again
Until in you, Christ be shaped.

4:20 I wish I could be with you now
And to change my voice's tone
Since in your particular case
Uncertainties I still own.

4:21 You who wish to be under law,
Answer me this one question:
Aren't you listening to the Law?
Let me your memory freshen.*

4:22 It's been written that Abraham
Had two sons eventually:
One son came by a woman slave,
The other by her who's free.

4:23 But the son from the slave woman,
By sinful flesh, he was born,
And the son from her who was free,
By a promise *God had sworn.

4:24 These things form an allegory,
For these women represent
The state of freedom or slavery,[179]
Each a type of covenant.

Hagar, who gave birth for slavery,
This woman does typify
The covenant that was given*
From the mountain called Sinai.

4:25 So this Hagar is Mount Sinai.
In Arabia, it is found.
She lines up with Jerusalem now,
For with her children she's bound.

4:26 But there's also Jerusalem,
Not this one but another,*
The one from above that's freedom,
And this one is our mother.

4:27 For it's been written in Scripture:
"O barren woman, rejoice!
You, woman, who does not give birth,
Break out and shout with your voice.

"For there are many more children
That are of the wilderness
Than the children of the woman
Who a husband does possess."

4:28 But you yourselves, my dear brothers,
Are children that correlate
To Isaac, *the promised child.
You're children of promise, I state.

4:29 But the one born by sinful flesh
Was persecuting away
He who was born of the Spirit,
And this still happens today.

4:30 But "Cast out the slave and her son,"
The Scripture does declare
Because with the free woman's son
He will never be coheir.

4:31 So, then in conclusion, brothers,
We are not children, *you see,
Of the woman who is a slave
But of the woman who's free.

5:1 Therefore, stand firm in this freedom
In which Christ has set us free,
And don't subject yourselves again
To a yoke of slavery.

5:2 Listen! I, Paul, am telling you:
If you receive circumcision,
As for Christ benefiting you,
There will be no provision.

5:3 And so again I testify
To each person who receives
The cutting called* circumcision,
An obligation this leaves.

That one must keep the entire Law,
Not a single part rejected.*
5:4 You who work to be righteous in law,
From Christ you're disconnected.

Yes, from Christ you're disconnected.
You've fallen from grace's state.
5:5 For it's in the Holy Spirit
That for hope we eagerly wait.

To be declared righteous by faith
Is the hope for which we wait,
Not a hope that is uncertain
But one we anticipate.[180]

5:6 For to be circumcised or not,
In Jesus Christ, both lack strength.
Only a faith that works through love
Has a force of any length.*

5:7 You were running so very well.
Who cut in and hindered your course
Of being convinced by the truth?
5:8 He who calls you was not the source.

5:9 You know that* just a little yeast
Causes the whole batch to rise.
5:10 That you'll think upon nothing else
I'm confident in the Lord's eyes.

But the one who is troubling you,
Whoever that one may be,
Will most certainly have to bear
The judgment ◆and penalty.

5:11 If I preach that circumcision
By all men must be employed,*
Why am I still persecuted?
The cross's offense would be void.

5:12 I could just about make the wish[181]
That the ones troubling you all
Would just emasculate themselves.
5:13 For in freedom was your call.

Only do not use that freedom
As a way to arm the flesh,
But keep serving one another
Through love. *This does refresh.

5:14 For the entire Law is fulfilled
In just this single command:
"Love your neighbor as yourself."
It's an unselfish demand.◆

5:15 But if biting one another
And devouring be resumed,
Watch out that by one another
You don't end up being consumed!

5:16 But I tell you, keep on living
By the Spirit *who's within,
And you'll by no means carry out
The fleshly desires *called sin.

5:17 For the sinful flesh desires things
That the Spirit does oppose,
And the Spirit desires things
That the flesh regards as foes.

For these two oppose each other
With this purpose to inspire:
That you not practice anything
That you happen to desire.

5:18 But assuming you're being led
By the Spirit *who has no flaw,
Then you truly are not under
The authority of law.

5:19 Now all the works which are produced
By the flesh are very plain,
And here's a list of some of them
Which I don't need to explain:*

Fornication, impurity,
As well as sensual pleasure,
5:20 Idolatry and sorcery,
And enmity without measure.[182]

Strife and unrighteous[183] jealousy,
Outbursts of uncontrolled wrath,
Selfish-ambitions and dissensions,
Pursuits of a factious path.

5:21 Acts of envy and drunkenness,
Feastings that honor some god,[184]
And other actions such as these
That we plainly can't applaud.*

As I told you previously,
I forewarn you; *I declare it:
That those who practice things like these,
God's kingdom they won't inherit.

5:22 The fruit produced by the Spirit
Is in contrast to these ways.
It is unselfish love and joy;
Peace and patience it displays.

It's kindness, goodness, faithfulness,
5:23 Gentleness and self-control.
Against such things, there is no law.
These virtues all do extoll.*

5:24 But all those who belong to Christ,
The flesh they have crucified
With its passions and its desires.
The fleshly self has died.[185]

5:25 So if we live by the Spirit,
Let's follow Him, *no other.
5:26 Don't fall to pride by challenging
Or envying one another.

6:1 Brothers, even if a person
Is caught in a sin of some kind,
You spiritual ones restore such one
With a gentleness of mind.

When any of you try this task
Of a brother's restoration,*
Keep a close eye on your own self
So you don't fall to temptation.

6:2 Carry one another's burdens.
This lifestyle *is to be sought,
For in that way you will fulfill
The law of love which Christ taught.[186]

6:3 For if anyone is something,
At least that's what he's believing,
When he's really nothing at all,
Himself he's just deceiving.

6:4 But let each one keep on testing
His own work *and no other,
Then he'll boast of himself alone
Without reference to another.

6:5 For each one must bear his own load,
6:6 But let the one taught the word
Participate in all good things
With the instructor, he has heard.

6:7 Stop being continually deceived.
No mocking of God will keep,
For whatever a person sows,
He will eventually reap.

6:8 For the one who keeps on sowing
To his own fleshly seduction
Will from these seeds of sinful flesh
Only harvest corruption.

But the one who sows to the Spirit,
And this lifestyle *he does keep,
From that same Holy Spirit
Eternal life will he reap.

6:9 Now let us who practice the good
Not give in to evil's fight,[187]
For in due time we'll surely reap
If we don't tire *of what's right.

6:10 So, as we have opportunity,
Let's work good toward all, *not wrong,
Especially toward the members who
To the household of faith belong.

6:11 Look! In large letters by my hand
To you all, I am writing.
6:12 There are those who in sinful flesh
Wish to look good by inciting –

Inciting you to be circumcised
That this be instituted:
That in relation to Christ's cross
They not be persecuted.

6:13 For not even these circumcised ones
Keep the Law to the utmost,[188]
But want you to be circumcised
So in your flesh, they can boast.

6:14 But may I never boast at all
Except in this thing alone,
The cross of the Lord Jesus Christ
Through which this has been shown:*

Through the Lord's cross the world to me
Has been truly crucified;
And through the Lord's cross to the world
I have been nailed ◆and I've died.

6:15 For circumcision means nothing,
Nor to be uncircumcised,
But to be a new creation
Is what should be emphasized.*

6:16 All who line up with this standard,
Upon them, God's peace does trod,[189]
As well as the mercy of Christ.
It's upon the Israel of God.

6:17 From this time on let no one cause
Any more trouble for me,
For I carry in my body
The brand of Jesus *you see.

6:18 The grace of our Lord Jesus Christ,
I now exclaim once again[190]
That it's with your spirit, brothers.
And that is the truth.[191] Amen.

THE POETIC LETTER TO THE EPHESIANS

1:1 Paul, an apostle of Christ Jesus
By God's will *being applied,
To the saints ◆who are set apart,
Who in Ephesus[192] reside.

But I do not write this letter*
Only to you who live there*
But also to the faithful saints
In Christ Jesus *everywhere.

1:2 To all of you *I write these words:
Grace and peace on you are poured,[193]
Which is from God our Father
And from Jesus Christ the Lord.

1:3 Blessings to the God and Father
Of Jesus Christ our Lord.
In the unseen place[194] that's in Christ,
Blessings on us God has poured.

Yes, every spiritual blessing
He has poured on us in Christ.
Blessings to our God and Father*
For these gifts that can't be priced.*

1:4 For before the world's creation
The Creator* God did choose
Us to be holy and blameless
In Christ through whom He views.

1:5 He predestined us for adoption
In a love *without measure
To Himself through Jesus the Christ,
Matching His will's good pleasure.

1:6 This all results in the praise
To the glory of His grace
Which he freely gifted to us
In His beloved *whom we embrace.

1:7 In His beloved we do possess
The redemption through His blood,
The forgiveness of sins, which match
The gracious riches *that flood.

1:8 For upon us He lavished them
In all wisdom and insight
1:9 At the time He made known to us
The mystery of His delight.

This did match His own good pleasure
Which in Himself He had willed
1:10 To manage all of the events
As to when they'd be fulfilled.

This was so that all things might find
In Christ their full summation.
The things in heaven and on earth
In Christ find harmonization.

1:11 Also in Christ, we, by His plan,
An inheritance did acquire
Who works all things according to
The firm counsel of His desire.

1:12 This was so that we who were first[195]
To have placed in Christ our hope
Would bring all praise to His glory
And bring Him into your scope.*

1:13 And so in Him you also hoped
When the message of truth you heard,
The good news of your salvation,
Receiving the truth of God's word.

As soon as you believed in Him,
With God's own seal you were sealed
With the promised Holy Spirit,
1:14 God's pledge of a future revealed -

The pledge of our inheritance
Until that day we're redeemed
As God's possession, resulting in
His glory being esteemed.

1:15 Because of this, after hearing
About your faith in the Lord[196]
And about your unselfish love
Which all the saints it is toward -

1:16 I don't stop giving thanks for you.
I keep giving thanks, I say,*
As I keep remembering you
Each and every time I pray.

1:17 I pray our Lord Jesus Christ's God,
The Father of exaltation,
Give you a spirit in knowing Him
Of wisdom and revelation.

1:18 For by this the eyes of your heart
Are enlightened for you to know
What is our hope, what is God's wealth,
And what His power does show.

I pray that you will come to know*
The hope that His calling paints
And the glorious wealth in this,
His inheritance in the saints -

1:19 And the surpassing greatness shown
By His power to us who believe
In accordance with the working
That His mighty strength does achieve.

1:20 This power He has worked in Christ
By raising Him from death's grip,
Seating Him in heaven[197] at His right,
Giving Him supreme headship.*

1:21 He's above all rule and power,
Lordship and authority,
Above all names named in this age
And in the age yet to be.

1:22 God has put into subjection
Everything under His feet.
God gave to the church Christ as head.
Head over all is His seat.[198]

1:23 The church is the body of Christ.
With His own self, it is filled.
He fills all things in all places,
Being over all as God willed.*

2:1 And in your sins and trespasses
You were all spiritually dead.
2:2 In them you used to live your lives,
The same way this world does head.

You lived just as the ruler
Of the realm of the air did will.
In the sons that disobey God
This spiritual ruler works still.

2:3 We all once lived among these sons
In the fleshly lusts instilled,
Doing the things the sinful flesh
And the sinful mind had willed.

And we by our very nature
Were children under God's wrath
Like the remainder of the world
Who live in that sinful path.*

2:4 But God who is rich in mercy,
2:5 Though in our sins we were dead,
Since He loved us with His great love,
He made us alive instead.

We're alive together with Christ,
For you have been saved by grace.
2:6 God raised us, seating us together
With Christ in the unseen place.[199]

2:7 This is so throughout the future
He might show *in a way sufficed
The surpassing wealth of His grace
In His goodness to us in Christ.

2:8 For by grace you've been saved through faith,
And from you, this did not come.
It's not by works; it's a gift from God
2:9 So no boasting can be done.

2:10 For in Christ we're His workmanship.
For good works we were created.
God prearranged that in these works
Our lives be navigated.

2:11 Therefore, recall who you once were,
Gentiles in the flesh, ◆by race.
You were called "the uncircumcised."
Circumcision had no place.*

You were called "the uncircumcised"
By "thc circumcised," as they say,
Which is a cutting of the flesh
By human hands anyway.

2:12 Recall that you were without Christ
In that time, ◆that duration,
Being estranged from citizenship
In the Israelite nation.

To the covenants of promise
You were strangers, *yes, you all,
Having no hope and without God
In this world, as you recall.

2:13 However, now in Christ Jesus,
You who were once far away
Have drawn near in the blood of Christ,
2:14 For He is our peace, *I say.

For He made both groups into one.
In His flesh, He demolished
The middle wall of division.
Hostility He abolished.

2:15 He did this by making useless
The Law of commands and decrees
To create the two in Himself
As one new man, making peace.

2:16 Also to reconcile both groups
To God in one body *that's new
By destroying through the cross
Hostility between the two.

2:17 When He came, He preached the good news
Of peace to those who were near
And to you who were far away
For Jew and Gentile to hear.*

2:18 For now, it is through Jesus Christ
That access we now possess
In one Spirit to the Father,
Both ♦Jew and Gentile, I stress.

2:19 So then, as strangers and aliens
You are no longer *enrolled.
You're co-citizens with the saints
And members of God's household.

2:20 For as a building you were built
On this foundation *alone,
Of the apostles and prophets
With Christ Jesus, the cornerstone.

2:21 In Christ the entire building,
Since it's joined in one accord,
Grows into a sanctuary
That is holy in the Lord.

2:22 You too are being built together
In Christ as God's dwelling place
Who lives in the Spirit among you
As you gather in one place.*

3:1 For this reason, I, who am Paul,
A prisoner for Christ *and His word
For the sake of all you Gentiles -
3:2 Now I'm assuming that you've heard.

That you've heard of the stewardship
Of the free gift◆ of God's grace
Which was given to me *by Him
For you all, ◆the Gentile race.

3:3 It's the mystery made known to me
By means of revelation
Just as I wrote about before
With little explanation.

3:4 When you read about this again,
You'll be able to understand
My insight into the mystery
Of Christ *revealed by God's hand.

3:5 For the mystery was not made known
In other generations
To any of the sons of men,
But now *there's revelations.

It's now revealed in the Spirit
To these that belong to God:
The holy apostles and prophets,
Who now make it known abroad.*

3:6 This way Gentiles can join as heirs
And share in the body *with Jews,
Also, partake of the promise
In Christ Jesus through the good news.

3:7 To this I became a servant
By the free gift of God's grace,
By the working of His power
As I go from place to place.*

3:8 This very grace was given me,
The very least of all the saints,
To preach to Gentiles the good news
Of Christ's wealth which no mind acquaints.

3:9 Also to bring to light the plan,
The mystery which from the start
Had been hidden in God Himself
Who created all things, *each part.

3:10 This way God's manifold wisdom
Could now through the church be made known
To rulers and authorities
Who in the unseen[200] *have their throne.

3:11 This *wisdom published through the church
Was all in perfect accord
With the eternal plan He made
In Jesus Christ our Lord.

3:12 In Him bold access with confidence
Through faith in Him we acquire.
3:13 My sufferings for you are your glory.
So I ask, in them don't tire.

3:14 - So for this reason, I myself
Before the Father bend my knees
3:15 From whom in heaven and on earth
Are named all its families.

3:16 I pray that from His glorious wealth
Power to you He would give
To be strengthened through His Spirit
In the inner self *to live.

3:17 The end would be that, through your faith
Of depending on His power,*
Christ would truly dwell in your hearts
Each and every hour.*

Since in the sphere of selfless love
Your roots have been planted deep,
Or, to put it another way,
Love is the foundation you keep -

3:18 I then pray that with all the saints
You'd be able to grasp love's breadth,
To grasp its length, also its height,
As well as to grasp its depth.

3:19 I pray that you would be able
To realize Christ's love *instilled
Which surpasses understanding
So with all God's fullness, you're filled.

3:20 Now to Him, the One who's able
With the power He works within
To do far above all we ask,
Far above all we imagine -

3:21 To Him be the glory ♦and praise
For all generations, then,
In the church and in Christ Jesus
Forever and ever. Amen.

4:1 Therefore, I, the chained in the Lord,
Urge you to live in a way
That measures up to the calling
By which you were called *that day.[201]

4:2 Do this in a loving manner
By bearing with one another,
Yet having all humility
And gentleness toward the other.

4:3 Do this by being diligent
To keep yourselves unified,
Chained together in harmony
With the Spirit *as your guide.

4:4 There's one body and one Spirit,
Just as also you were called
In the sphere of one single hope
That your calling has installed.

4:5 One Lord, one faith, one baptism,
4:6 One God and Father of all,
Who is over, operates through,
And resides among us all.

4:7 However, to each one of us
Was given grace in accord
With the measure of the gifting
Apportioned by Christ *our Lord.

4:8 For it says, "When He ascended
Into the high place, He led
Captives into captivity,
And gifts to mankind He spread."

4:9 Now what does "ascended" imply?
But that He made a descent
Into a depth ◆below the earth.
Lower than the earth He went.[202]

4:10 He who descended is also
He who went up *by God's will,
Rising above all the heavens
So that all things He might fill. [203]

4:11 Christ Himself gave the apostles,
And the evangelists *who preach,
And the prophets *who prophesy,
As well as the pastors who teach -

4:12 He gave them to equip the saints
For a work of serving *others
For the purpose of building up
The body of Christ, *my brothers.

4:13 And this 'til the oneness of faith
And of God's Son as fully known,
We all attain, picturing us
As a man who is fully grown.

However not just any man,*
But a man who can be seen,*
Measuring to the height of Christ,
His fullness of growth, *I mean.

4:14 This is so that little children
We might no longer remain,
Being tossed and carried about
By every windy campaign.

That's to say, the doctrine of men
Must not have our reception.*
They teach in cunning trickery
For a scheme of deception.

4:15 But this is so that we might grow
As in love the truth we spread,
Growing in every way in Him,
In Christ who is the head.

4:16 From Him the entire body
Is joined together and held
By every joint that is supplied
So that it may be propelled.*

Propelled by the proper measure
Of each part working thereof,
Thus causing the body to grow,
Edifying itself in love.

4:17 Therefore, I affirm in the Lord,
Saying your life must be defined
No longer by how pagans live
In an emptiness of their mind.

4:18 They've been darkened in their thinking,
Estranged from the life God imparts
Because of the ignorance within,
Because of their hardened hearts.

4:19 They've given themselves to lewdness,
Fully calloused *in each deed,
Ending up doing every kind
Of impurity with greed.

4:20 But you did not learn Christ this way,
4:21 Assuming of Him you've heard,
Assuming you were taught in Him
Since in Jesus is truth's word.

4:22 You were taught to strip the old man,
The old life you used to live,
For the old man is corrupted
By lusts that deceit does give.

4:23 And you were taught to be renewed
In your attitude of mind.
4:24 You were taught to put on the new,
The man who's being designed.

The new man is being created
According to God to live
In righteousness and piety,
The character truth does give.

4:25 Therefore, having stripped off falsehood,
Each of you with your *brother,
Since he's your neighbor, speak just truth.
We're members of one another.

4:26 Be angry *in a righteous way,
And don't let sin show its face.
Don't let the sun set on your anger.
4:27 Don't give the Devil a place.

4:28 Let the one who steals stop stealing.
Let him toil *and not be greedy,
Working good with his hands to have
Something to share with the needy.

4:29 Let no foul word come from your mouth.
Only good words volunteer,
Words that build up for what's needed
To give grace to those who hear.

4:30 And don't grieve God's Holy Spirit,
By which Spirit you were sealed
For the day of full redemption
When all God's own is revealed.[204]

4:31 Let all bitterness and anger,
Wrath, clamor, and evil talk
Be put away from all of you
With each kind of evil walk.

4:32 And be kind to one another,
Having a compassion too,
Forgiving each one even as
God in Christ forgave you.

5:1 Therefore, as children dearly loved,
Imitators of God become.
5:2 Live a lifestyle in selfless love
Even as Christ has done.

Christ loved us and gave Himself up.
In our place *He Himself stood
As an offering and sacrifice
Rising to God smelling good.

5:3 Now regarding fornication,
All impurity, or greed,
These must be unnamed among you
Just as befits saints indeed.

5:4 Also filthy and foolish talk,
Or jesting with crude oration.
All such speech does not befit saints,
Rather gracious conversation.[205]

5:5 For you all know this to be true:
All whom *God identifies
As a fornicator, as impure,
Or as one with covetous eyes –

(Coveting is idolatry)
You know *their true recompense.
In the kingdom of God and Christ
They have no inheritance.

5:6 Let none deceive you by vain words,
For due to these acts of offense,
God's wrath is coming on the sons
Marked by disobedience.

5:7 So, don't become partners with them,
5:8 For you were at one time dark,
But in connection with the Lord
Now light has become your mark.

Lead lives as children marked by light,
5:9 For the fruit produced by light
Is evident in every kind
Of good, of truth, and of right.

5:10 Lead lives as children marked by light
In the examination
Of what's well-pleasing to the Lord
With personal application.*

5:11 And do not participate in
The fruitless works of the dark.
Instead, reprove these fruitless works,
5:12 For it's shameful to just remark.◆

The secret things done by them,
To just talk of them is not right.
5:13 But all the things that are reproved
Are made evident by the light.

5:14 For all that's shown becomes lit up,
For it says: "Rise, sleepy head,
And upon you, the Christ will shine.
Rise up from among the dead."

5:15 Therefore, with care watch how you live,
Not as unwise but as wise,
5:16 Buying up opportunity,
For of evil the days comprise.

5:17 Because of this, don't be foolish,
But perceive what is the Lord's will,
5:18 And do not become drunk by wine
Since with wildness it does fill.

Instead, keep on being filled up
With the Spirit *who will impel;
5:19 Speak to others in psalms and hymns
And spiritual songs as well.

Sing and play music to the Lord,
Making sure it's* in your heart;
5:20 Always give thanks for everything
That to us God does impart.*

Thank God the Father in the name
Of Jesus Christ our Lord;
5:21 Submit yourselves to one another,
With the fear of Christ outpoured.

5:22 Wives, submit to your own husbands
As to the Lord you submit
5:23 Since a man is head of his wife
Just like Christ as head does sit.

Jesus* Christ is head of the church,
His body, *as I have said,
Of which He Himself is Savior.
A body submits to the head.*

5:24 But the point is that[206] as the church
Submits to Christ as its head,
So to your husbands in all things
You wives submit, *as I've said.

5:25 Husbands, love your wives selflessly
As Christ loved the church this way.
He gave Himself up in her place
For this to be His display:*

5:26 First,* that He might sanctify her
(Set apart this word does mean),*
Washing with water in the word,
Thus making her very clean.

5:27 Second,* that He present to Himself
A glorious church without stain,
Without wrinkle or any such thing,
Just holy and without blame.

5:28 Thus husbands must love their own wives
As they love their bodies they tend.[207]
He who selflessly loves his wife,
To himself that love does extend.

5:29 For no one ever hates his flesh,
But he nurtures it with care
Just as also Christ does the church
5:30 Since in His body we share.[208]

5:31 That's why a man must leave the home
Of his father and mother
And be united to his wife,
To be one flesh with each other.

5:32 This mystery is very profound,
Once hidden from anyone's search.[209]
Now I'm speaking of the mystery
Regarding Christ and the church.

5:33 However, each and every man
Must as himself love his wife,
And she must respect her husband,
For this is the marriage life.*

6:1 Children, in the sphere of the Lord
Obey your parents. It's right.
6:2 "Honor your father and mother"
Is the commandment that *I cite.

It's the first one with a promise:
6:3 "That with you all may go well,
And a long life you might enjoy
On the earth in which you dwell."

6:4 Parents,[210] concerning your children,
To anger do not incite.
In the Lord's training and warning
Raise them up, *for that is right.

6:5 Slaves obey your earthly masters
In a fear and trembling way,
With sincerity from your heart
Just as Christ you would obey.

6:6 Do not obey just to please men,
Being concerned with what they see,
But as Christ's slaves who do God's will
From the heart you are to be.

6:7 As to the Lord and not to men,
Serve with a good attitude
6:8 Since you know that one will receive
From the Lord *by what He's viewed.

Whatever good anyone does,
He will receive from the Lord
(Whether he be a slave or free)
That same good as a reward.

6:9 Masters, do the same thing toward them.
Give up threatening, for you know
Your mutual Lord is in heaven.
Partialness He does not show.

6:10 Finally, be strong in the Lord
And in His powerful might.
6:11 Put on the whole armor of God
So that you can stand upright.

Stand against all the strategies
Of the Devil *in his schemes,
6:12 For it's not against blood and flesh
That we struggle *as it seems.

It's against rulers, authorities,
Spiritual powers, *I mean,
Powers that rule this world's darkness,
Evil spirits in the unseen.[211]

6:13 Due to this, take up God's armor
To withstand in the evil day,
And after accomplishing all,
In that same firm stand to stay.

6:14 Therefore, stand by wearing in truth
A belt wrapped around your waist,
And by putting on the breastplate,
The righteousness *you've embraced.

6:15 Stand with sandals strapped to your feet
Always in preparation
Of sharing the gospel of peace,
Of reconciliation.◆

6:16 Above all, hold the shield of faith
In your hands firmly clenched*
So that all the flaming arrows
Of the evil one can be quenched.

6:17 Stand by putting on the helmet,
The helmet of salvation,
And stand holding the Spirit's sword,
God's word *of revelation.

6:18 Keep on praying with every kind
Of prayer and petition
On every kind of occasion
In the Spirit's *disposition.

And for this keep on the alert
With a persevering heart
And with every kind of petition
For all the ones set apart.[212]

6:19 And pray for me that words be given
When opening my mouth I choose
So that I might boldly make known
The mystery of the good news.

6:20 I am on behalf of this news
An ambassador in a chain.
Pray I speak boldly as required
When the gospel I explain.

6:21 Now my dear brother, Tychicus,
A faithful servant in the Lord,
Will let you know all that I face,
Also all that I afford.

6:22 To you all I am sending him.
For this *from us he departs:
That you might know of our affairs,
And he might counsel your hearts.

6:23 Both peace and love along with faith
Is to the brothers, I exclaim.[213]
From God our Father and His Christ,
The Lord Jesus, *these gifts came.

6:24 All who love our Lord Jesus Christ
In a way that will not die,
The undeserved free gift of◆ grace[214]
Is with them *in full supply!

THE POETIC LETTER TO THE PHILIPPIANS

1:1 Paul and Timothy, Christ's[215] bond slaves,
To all Christ's saints[216] in Philippi
With overseers and deacons,
This epistle we supply.*

1:2 To all of you we write these words:*
Grace and peace on you are poured,[217]
Which proceed from God our Father
And from Jesus Christ the Lord.

1:3 Every time I remember you,
Thanks to my God I relay;
1:4 In every prayer of mine for you
With joy, I do always pray.

1:5 It's based on your contribution
From the first day 'til today
Toward the gospel *that's being preached.
So, of this I'm convinced to say:

1:6 I'm convinced that He who began
A good work in you, each one,
Will complete it until the day
Of Jesus the Christ, *God's Son.

1:7 It's right that I think this of you
Since I have you in my heart,
Because all of you in this grace
Along with me, share a part.

In my chains of imprisonment
With me you participate.
In the gospel, you share with me
As I defend and validate.

1:8 For I constantly long for you all
With the affection Jesus[218] shows.
God is my witness as to how
Deep that desire really goes.*

1:9 I pray this: that your love abound
More and more in all insight
And in full knowledge *of the Lord
1:10 That you may discern what's right.

And I pray this concerning you:*
That you become genuine
Without a mixture of offense
'Til the day of Christ comes in.

1:11 This comes from being fully filled
With the fruit righteousness brings
Which is through Jesus Christ alone
So God's praise and glory rings.

1:12 But I determine that you learn
That what has happened to me
Has, my brothers, instead advanced
The gospel *for more to see.

1:13 For my chains that are due to Christ
Have become very well-known
Among the entire palace guard
And to all the rest *in Rome.[219]

1:14 And more who've trusted in the Lord
By the chains upon me here,
These brothers have far more courage
To speak the word without fear.

1:15 Yet although some are preaching Christ
Out of envy and discord,
Some are preaching out of goodwill
That Jesus* Christ *is Lord.

1:16 Yes, these ones are proclaiming Christ
From love ◆with no selfish views
Since they know that I'm appointed
To defend the gospel news.

1:17 The others preach Christ from motives
That are selfish and impure,
For they think that it will raise up
Pressure in my chains for sure.

1:18 What then? Except in every way,
Whether in truth or deceit,
I'm glad that Christ is being preached,
But my joy will be complete.

1:19 For I know that this will turn out
For my release through your prayer
As the Spirit of Christ Jesus
Gives provision for my care.

1:20 This is all in accordance with
My hope and expectation.
I also know that in nothing
Will shame be my inclination.

But in all boldness Christ will be,
As has always been and is now,
Magnified in my own body
Through my life or death somehow.

1:21 For if I live, it is for Christ,
And if I die, it's my gain.
1:22 If I keep living in this flesh,
Fruitful work I will sustain.

Which I prefer, I do not know,
1:23 But I am torn between the two.
I have the desire to depart
And be with Christ. *It's true.

And while it is far more better
For my death to be my gain,
1:24 It is more needed for your sake
That in this flesh I remain.

1:25 Convinced of this, I know I'll stay.
With you all, I'll continue
For both your joy and advancement
Of the faith *that's within you.

1:26 This is so that your boast in me
May in Christ Jesus abound
Through my return visit to you.
Yes, may pride in Christ resound.*

1:27 Only live as a citizen
In a way that shows the worth
Of the good news about the Christ
While you live here on the earth.*

I command this so that whether
I come to you and appear,
Or if I am away from you,
These things of you I might hear:

That in one spirit you're standing firm,
And with your thinking the same
You're striving together for the faith
That the gospel does proclaim.

1:28 And that, as to those who oppose,
You have no trepidation,
Which is a sign of their destruction
But a sign of your salvation.

1:29 And this is from God since He gave
Freely for Christ's sake to you
Not only to believe in Him
But to suffer for Him too.

1:30 You are having the same struggle
Which you witnessed in my case,
Which you now hear happening to me,
One chained in this prison space.*

2:1 So, if there's any counsel in Christ,
Or any comfort from love,
Or any kind of fellowship
In the Spirit *from above -

If there is any compassion,
Or mercies of any kind,
2:2 Then bring my joy to completion
So you think with the same mind.

This comes from having the same love.
A selfless love we must bring,◆
While we all with united souls
Keep thinking on the same thing.

2:3 Do nothing from self-ambition
Or according to empty pride,
2:4 But consider one another
With humility applied.

Regard as higher than yourselves
One another by noting
The interests which others possess.
Just yours don't be promoting.

2:5 Think in this way within yourselves
As was in Christ Jesus too
2:6 Who was existing in God's form,
But did not keep that in view.◆

Although existing in God's form,
The privilege He did not hold
Of His equality with God,
2:7 But instead this did unfold:*

He emptied Himself *of privilege.
He then took a bond slave's form,
Becoming in mankind's likeness,
As in this world, He was born.*

2:8 And having been found as a man
In His outward appearance,
He humbled Himself *to His God
In absolute adherence.*

Yes, He became obedient
Without thought of His own loss,*
All the way to the point of death,
Even death upon a cross.

2:9 So, God highly exalted Him.
Far above all He became,*
And then freely bestowed on Him
A name above every name.

2:10 That way in the name of Jesus
To Him will bow every knee,
Whether in heaven or on earth
Or under the earth they be.

2:11 Also every tongue will confess
That Jesus Christ is Lord,
Resulting in all the glory
On Father God being poured.

2:12 Therefore then, my dearly loved ones,
As you've always obeyed *what's taught -
Not just when I'm present with you
But now much more when I'm not –

Keep working out your salvation
With fear and trembling within,
2:13 For in you God works both the wish
And the power to please Him.

2:14 No complaining and arguing
In anything that you do
2:15 In order that you might become
Blameless and pure *through and through.

Be children of God without fault
In an evil universe,*
In the midst of a generation
That is crooked and perverse.

You appear as lights in the world
Among this generation
2:16 By holding firm the word of life
As your illumination.*

Then I will have reason to boast
In the day Christ returns *to earth
Because I did not run in vain
Nor was my toil without worth.

2:17 But although[220] as a drink offering
I myself am being outpoured
On the sacrifice and service
Produced by your faith *in the Lord –

Although this is true, I rejoice,
And I rejoice with you all.
2:18 Likewise, you also must rejoice.
So, rejoice with me, *with Paul.

2:19 Now I hope in the Lord Jesus
To send you Timothy soon
So that when I learn of your state,
With cheer, I might resume.

2:20 For I've no one as like-minded
Who will genuinely care
For all the things concerning you.
Of no one I am aware.◆

2:21 For all are seeking their own interests
And not those of Jesus Christ,
2:22 But you all know his proven worth
As one who has sacrificed.*

As a child would serve a father,
So also with me, he's served
For the purpose of the gospel.
His worth you know. You've observed.[221]

2:23 So, I hope to send right away
This one to your location
As soon as I can look away
From my own situation.

2:24 But I am convinced in the Lord
That soon I will also come,
2:25 But I deem it necessary
To now send this other one:

Ephaphroditus, my brother,
Coworker, and soldier indeed,
But your apostle whom you sent[222]
As a servant to my need.

2:26 For he was longing for you all
And became very distressed
Because you heard that he was ill,
2:27 For close to death he progressed.

But God had mercy upon him,
Me also, not him alone,
So that a pile of grief on grief
Would not upon me be thrown.

2:28 Therefore, to you I'm sending him
Much more eagerly, *I stress,
For your joy when you see him again,
And for my grief to be less.

2:29 Therefore, welcome him in the Lord.
Receive him with joy complete,
And everyone who is like him
With the highest honor treat.

2:30 He nearly died for Christ's work's sake
Risking his own life *at will
To supply in service to me
What you all could not fulfill.

3:1 Furthermore, rejoice in the Lord.
To write the same things for me
Is not wearisome, my brothers.
It's for your security.

3:2 Beware of the dogs *as they're called;
Beware of the false incision;
Beware of the evil workers,
For we are the circumcision.

3:3 Yes, we are the circumcision*
Who serve by God's Spirit *inside,
Who make our boast in Christ Jesus,
And do not in the flesh confide.

3:4 I myself in the flesh possess
Reasons to confide, although.
If anyone else thinks to trust
In the flesh, then I more so.

3:5 I was circumcised on day eight;
I'm from the Israelite race;
I'm from the tribe of Benjamin,
A Hebrew of Hebrews my place.

As to the measurement of law,
I became a Pharisee;
3:6 As to zeal, a persecutor
Of the church, I came to be.

As to righteous standards in law,
I became without mistake.
3:7 But the things that were gain to me,
I deemed as loss for Christ's sake.

3:8 But even more than all of this,
All things as loss I now deem
Since knowing Christ Jesus my Lord
Is surpassingly supreme.

Because of Christ, I suffered loss
Of all things *that gave me my name.
As rubbish I considered them
In order that Christ I might gain.

3:9 I also ◆deemed them as rubbish
So that in Him I might be found,
Not having my own righteousness
With Jewish law[223] as its ground.

But ◆that in Him I might be found
With what is through faith in Christ,
The righteousness that comes from God
With faith as the ground sufficed.

3:10 I considered all things rubbish◆
So that Him I might come to know
As well as the mighty power
That His resurrection did show.

Even sharing in His sufferings,
Conforming to how He died
3:11 So that my rising from the dead
I might somehow get supplied.

3:12 Not that I've now received it all
Or have now come to perfection,
But I pursue, knowing all this,
So that I might *have direction.

The direction of* grabbing hold
Of that for which Christ grabbed me.
3:13 And I, brothers, do not regard
That I've grabbed it completely.

But I regard to do one thing
As I remember no more
All the things which are behind
And strain toward what's set before:

3:14 I run toward the goal *set by God
For the prize that He'll extend,
Which is God calling me upward
In Christ Jesus *at the end.

3:15 Therefore, all those who are mature,
Let us dwell on this ideal.
If anyone thinks differently,
To him, this God will reveal.

3:16 Nevertheless, let us all live
With all progress being sustained[224]
According to the measure of growth
That we have already attained.

3:17 Brothers, join yourselves together
As imitators of me,
And observe the ones who live out
The example in us you see.

3:18 For many are walking about
Whom I often did expose,
But now I tell you while weeping,
To the cross of Christ, they're foes.

3:19 Their end is certain destruction;
Their god is their bellies *that swell;
And their glory is in their shame,
Whose minds on earthly things dwell.

3:20 For our citizenship exists
In heaven *(that's where it is stored),
From which we eagerly expect
The Savior, Jesus Christ the Lord.

3:21 He will take our present bodies
Which are in a humbled form.
Matching His glorious body,
He will change them to conform.

This process of transformation◆
Will be by the power He brings,
The working of His own power
To subject to Himself all things.

4:1 Therefore, my brothers, ◆whom I love,
My dear ones for whom I long,
You friends◆ who are my joy and crown,
In the Lord stand firm ◆and strong.

4:2 Now I urge both Euodia
And Syntyche in the task
Of thinking the same in the Lord.
4:3 True comrade, your help I ask.

Help them who toiled in the gospel
With me and Clement *without strife,
Also with all my coworkers
Whose names are in the book of life.

4:4 Rejoice in the Lord always.
Again, keep rejoicing I say.
4:5 Make your gentleness known to all.
The Lord's near, not far away.[225]

4:6 Don't worry about anything,
But in everything express,
By prayer and by petition
With thanks to God, your requests.

4:7 And your peace with God[226] which exceeds
The mind's whole capacity
Will in Christ Jesus guard your hearts
And minds ◆from anxiety.

4:8 Lastly, brothers, whatever's true,
Whatever's proper to love,
Whatever's noble, pure, or right,
Whatever's well-spoken of –

If there is anything at all
Which moral excellence brings
Or anything that's praiseworthy,
Let your mind dwell on these things.

4:9 And all that you learned and received
And heard and observed in me,
Practice them, and the God of peace
Will with you certainly be.

4:10 I rejoiced greatly in the Lord
That your concern for me revived.
Though you already were concerned,
No opportunity arrived.

4:11 I am not saying all these things
Because of a need *to present,
For in whatever state I am
I have learned to be content.

4:12 I know of having a little;
I know of having a lot;
In anything and everything
I have learned the secret *taught.

Whether I am filled or hungry,
Whether riches or need I see,
4:13 I am strong in all occasions
Through the One who strengthens me.

4:14 However, you did very well
In your participation,
By sharing with me while I was
In trials and◆ tribulation.

4:15 You also know, Philippians,
When the good news had its start,
When I left from Macedonia,
With me, only you took part.

In the giving and receiving
No other church shared in that deed.
4:16 Even in Thessalonica
You sent more than once for my need.

4:17 Not that I am seeking the gift,
But I'm seeking for the fruit
Which increases in your account.[227]
Riches it does constitute.

4:18 But I have received all payments,
And I am fully supplied.
I have been filled completely up
As your giving was applied.*

For 'twas from Epaphroditus
I received the things from you,
A pleasant smelling sacrifice
Which God had accepted too.

4:19 My God will fill your every need,
And this will be in accord
With the wealth He has in glory
In Jesus Christ *our Lord.

4:20 Now to God, who is our Father,
To Him is *again and again
All the glory forevermore.
To Him is the glory. Amen.[228]

4:21 Greet every saint in Christ Jesus.
No exception I declare.*
The brothers who are with me here
Send greetings to all you there.

4:22 All the saints ◆whom God set apart,
Send you their greetings, *I am told,
But particularly the ones
Who belong to Caesar's household.

4:23 The undeserved free gift of◆ grace
Which from the Lord Jesus Christ came
Is with your spirit *all the time!
This is a matter to exclaim.[229]

THE POETIC LETTER TO THE COLOSSIANS

1:1 Paul, apostle of Christ Jesus
By means of God's own delight,
And the brother called Timothy,
To you in Colossae we write.*

1:2 To you, brothers, faithful in Christ,
His saints ◆who are set apart.
God our Father to all of you
Both grace and peace did impart.[230]

1:3 To our Lord Jesus Christ's Father,
To God our thanks we're giving
All the time as we pray for you
1:4 Because of *how you're living.

We've heard about your faithfulness
In relation to Jesus Christ
And of your love toward all the saints,
A love that has sacrificed.[231]

1:5 Your actions are due to the hope
Which for you in heaven is stored,
About which you previously heard
In the message *about the Lord.

I'm speaking of the word of truth,
1:6 The gospel that to you came.
It's bearing fruit among all the world,
And growth it continues to gain.

Likewise, among you it's bearing fruit,
And it continues to grow
From the first day God's grace in truth
You heard and came to know.

1:7 For you learned it from Epaphras,
Our fellow bond slave and friend.
He's your faithful servant of Christ
Wherever him you might send.*

1:8 Epaphras also informed us
Of your love in the Spirit.
1:9 So, we've not stopped praying for you
From when we started to hear it.

From day one we have been praying
That the knowledge of His will
In spiritual insight and wisdom
Of all kinds might you infill.

1:10 We pray this so that you might walk
In a manner that reflects
The worth or value of the Lord,
To please Him in all respects.

You please the Lord by bearing fruit
In every work that is good
And by growing in knowing God,
Personally[232] *as you should.

1:11 By being strengthened in all power
Matching His glorious might
For all patience and endurance
With joy *in spite of the plight.

1:12 By giving thanks to the Father
Who qualified us to share
In the inheritance of the saints
In the light. *We're each an heir!

1:13 He rescued us from the power
That darkness on the world shoves,
And transferred us to the kingdom
That's ruled by the Son He loves.

1:14 In the Son we have been released
By the ransom that He paid.[233]
It's the forgiveness of our sins,
This redemption *that was made.

1:15 The Son is the image of God
Who's pure form no man can see.
He's firstborn over all creation;
He has all authority.[234]

1:16 All that's in heaven and on earth,
Both the seen and the unseen,
All these were created in Him.
That is why He is supreme.[235]

Whether there are thrones or lordships,
Rulers or authorities,
All have been created through Him
And for Him, *yes, all of these.

1:17 And so He is above all things,
And in Him all things consist.
1:18 He is the head of the body,
The church *which for Him does exist.

He's the beginning[236] in this sense,
The firstborn, ◆which means above all,
Derived from rising from the dead,[237]
That He might rank first among all.

1:19 For God was pleased to make in Christ
His complete fullness to dwell,
1:20 And through Christ to reconcile
All things to Himself as well.[238]

And so He makes peace through the blood
From the cross on which Christ *died.
To all things on earth or in heaven
This way the peace is applied.*

1:21 As for you, although at one time
You were completely estranged
And hostile-minded in evil works,
1:22 To reconcile God arranged.

God now reconciled you through death
In Christ's body, His fleshly frame,
To present you before Himself
As holy, with no fault or blame.

1:23 This, of course, makes the assumption
That in the faith you remain
Firmly established and steadfast,
Not moved from the hope •made plain -

The hope proclaimed by the gospel,
The good news• which you all heard.
To every creature under heaven
Has been announced this word.

I, Paul, have become a servant
To this gospel, •the good news.
1:24 In all my sufferings for your sake
To keep rejoicing I choose.

For Christ's afflictions in my flesh
Which lack *but must be hurled,
I complete for His body's sake,
The church •called out from the world.[239]

1:25 According to God's stewardship
On me and for you conferred,
A servant to the church I became
To fulfill God's mystery word.

1:26 This mystery which from ages past
Has been deeply concealed,
Hidden from past generations,
To His saints is now revealed.

1:27 God willed to make known to His saints
Among the Gentile nations
The glorious riches of this mystery
Hidden from past generations.*

This is the mystery: Christ in you;
The hope of glory is He.
1:28 We proclaim Him to every man
With the same consistency.*

We admonish and teach each one
In all wisdom, *I assure,
In order to present each man
In Jesus Christ as mature.

1:29 For this I'm also laboring,
Agonizing *every hour,
In accordance to His working
Which works in me with power.

2:1 For I wish you to know how great
A struggle for you I embrace,
And for the Laodiceans,
And for all who've not seen my face.

2:2 I share this to comfort their hearts
Being joined in love for these things:
All the wealth in the certainty
That understanding brings.

In other words, for the knowledge
That is personal and real,[240]
The knowledge of God's mystery,
Namely, Christ *whom we reveal.

2:3 In Christ are all the treasures hid.
Wisdom and knowledge are they.
2:4 I say this so that by winsome speech
No one might lead you astray.

2:5 For though I'm absent physically,
I am with you in spirit.
Your good conduct and firm faith in Christ
Gives me joy when I hear it.

2:6 Therefore, just as you first received
Jesus Christ as the Lord,
Continue on walking in Him
In this way that I record:*

2:7 Walk by being firmly planted
And built up in Him and growing,
Gaining strength in the faith as taught
With thankfulness overflowing.

2:8 Watch out so that there'll be no one
Who takes you as spoils of war
By means of their philosophy
And deceit which has no core.

For it is all patterned after
The traditions men have made
And after worldly principles,
Not after what Christ conveyed.

2:9 For in Him complete deity
Bodily dwells, as I've said,[241]
2:10 And you have been filled up in Him.
Of all rule and power He's head.

2:11 In Him you all were circumcised.
Without hands, the body was sliced[242]
In removing the sinful flesh,
A circumcision done by Christ.

2:12 For in baptism you, with Him,
Were buried and raised *by grace
Through faith in the working of God
Who raised Him from death's embrace.

2:13 Although you were spiritually dead
In your sins and in the drive
Of your own uncircumcised flesh,
With Christ, He made you alive.

He did this by forgiving us
All the transgressions we made,
2:14 By erasing from our account
The debt *we could not have paid.

This account contained the decrees
Set against us *for our loss,
Yet He's taken it from our midst
By nailing it to the cross.

2:15 After the spiritual rulers
And authorities were undressed,[243]
He boldly exposed them on it,
His triumph over them expressed.

2:16 Therefore, let no one be your judge
In regards to drink or food,
Or how a new moon or festival
Or Sabbath days should be viewed.

2:17 All these things are just a shadow
Of things about to arise,
But the body belongs to Christ.
2:18 Let none rob you of the prize.

Like one who delights in humbling
Himself to extreme degrees[244]
And in the worship of angels,
Who stands on visions he sees -[245]

Who with a mind set on his flesh,
Is puffed up with empty pride,
2:19 Who does not connect to the head
From whom the body is tied.◆

From the head the entire body,
Supplied and joined together
Through all its joints and ligaments,
In God increases its measure.

2:20 Assuming you have died with Christ
From worldly philosophies,
Why are you alive in the world,
Submitting to rules like these:

2:21 "Do not handle; don't taste or touch,"
2:22 Such things that decay with use?
These rules are just the commandments
And teachings that men produce.

2:23 Such teachings look reasonable
With a wisdom they compile
In a religion that's self-made
And in their self-denial.

A wisdom in bodily torture,
In self-humiliation,
Without any value against
Fleshly gratification.

3:1 Therefore, since you were raised with Christ,
Keep seeking *the things that aren't flawed,
The things above where Christ is now,
Seated at the right hand of God.

3:2 Keep focused on the things above,
Not earthly things. *It's forbidden.
3:3 For you died, and your life with Christ
In God has now been hidden.

3:4 When Christ, who is your life, appears,
No longer being concealed,*
Then you also along with Him
In glory will be revealed.

3:5 Therefore, as to these earthly things,
Put to death each body part:
Do not yield to fornication
Or evil lusts of the heart.

Do not yield to impurity
Or passion that's unrestrained.
Do not yield to covetousness,
For an idol, you'll have gained.

3:6 On account of these earthly things
God's wrath is coming someday.
3:7 You used to walk in all these things.
Living in them was your way.

3:8 But right now throw off all these things:
Wrath, rage, and acting mean;
Do not allow out of your mouth
Evil words or the obscene.

3:9 Stop lying to one another
Since the old self is now gone.
You stripped it with its practices,
3:10 And the new self you've put on.

The new self is being renewed
Into a knowledge that's true
According to the likeness of Him
Who created it in you.

3:11 In the new creation of God
No distinction is a thought.*
There's no such thing as Greek or Jew,
Or one circumcised or not.

No Barbarian or Scythian,
No slave or free, *no lists.
But Christ is everything to all,
And among all, He exists.

3:12 Therefore, as those chosen by God,
Dearly loved and set apart,
Put on a kind of compassion
That is truly from the heart.

Put on goodness, humility,
Patience and a spirit that's meek,
3:13 Putting up with one another,
And forgiveness you must speak.◆

If one complains about someone,
They must forgive each other.
Just as the Lord forgave you all,
Thus do to one another.

3:14 And upon all these put on love,
Which is the bond of perfection.
3:15 Let the peace of Christ keep ruling
In your hearts, *giving direction.

Into this peace, you all were called
In a body unified.
Be full of thanks and let Christ's word
3:16 Within you richly abide.

Teach and reprove one another
In wisdom with all its parts.
In psalms, hymns, and spiritual songs
Sing to God with thankful hearts.

3:17 Whatever you do in word or deed,
Do everything in the name
Of the Lord Jesus while through Him
Thanksgiving to God[246] you exclaim.

3:18 Women, submit to your husbands,
As in the Lord it's fitting.
3:19 Men, unselfishly love your wives,
All bitterness omitting.

3:20 You children, obey your parents,
Not in some things but* in all,
For this is pleasing to the Lord.
Obedience is His call.*

3:21 Parents,[247] don't provoke your children
To become stirred up or mad,
Otherwise, they'll be discouraged,
Disheartened◆ and never glad.*

3:22 Slaves, obey your earthly masters
In everything *without pause,
Not just serving well when they watch,
Or just to get men's applause.

But obey in sincerity,
One that is heartfelt ◆and sound,
Out of deep respect for the Lord
Regardless of who's around.*

3:23 Whatever work you are to do,
Let your soul in that work be poured,
Not as if you are serving men
But as if you're serving the Lord.

3:24 For you know that you will receive
From the Lord the true reward,
The heavenly inheritance.
Serve the Christ who is your Lord.

3:25 For the one who practices wrong
Will receive in reality
That which corresponds to the wrong
Without partiality.

4:1 Masters, grant justice and fairness
To your slaves, *no one ignored,
Since you know that you also have
A master in heaven, *the Lord.

4:2 Keep devoting yourselves to prayer
While in it keeping alert,
Connecting it with thanksgiving
4:3 While prayers for us you exert.

And beg God that an open door
To us for the word be gained
To speak the mystery of Christ,
For which also I've been chained.

4:4 Keep praying that I make it known
In an appropriate way,*
Speaking what is necessary,
What's required for me to say.◆

4:5 Toward those who are outside *the church,
In wisdom, you are to walk,
Buying up opportunity,
Being careful how you talk.*

4:6 Your speech must always be spoken
In grace, well-seasoned with salt,
So that you might know what's needed
To answer each one *without fault.

4:7 Tychicus, a much-loved brother,
A faithful servant *who cares,
A fellow bond slave in the Lord,
Will inform you of my affairs.

4:8 I'm sending you him for this cause:
That our circumstances you learn
And that he encourage your hearts.
With him this brother I return:[248]

4:9 Onesimus, who came from you,
A faithful brother who's dear.
Both of them will make known to you
All that is happening here.

4:10 Aristarchus sends you greetings,
A fellow prisoner of mine.
Mark, the cousin of Barnabas,
Greets you also at this time.

You're instructed to welcome Mark
Whenever to you he comes.
4:11 Jesus, called Justus, greets you too.
These two are the only ones -

These are the only coworkers
For God's kingdom *to be sent
Who are from the circumcision.
They became my encouragement.

4:12 Epaphras, who came from your group,
A greeting to you he sends.
This bond slave of Christ all the time
In his prayers for you contends.

He prays for you so you might stand
Mature and completely filled
In every single thing God wants.
Such toil in him is instilled.*

4:13 For I testify this of him:
That his toil is great for you,
For those in Laodicea,
And those in Hierapolis too.

4:14 Luke, the dear doctor, and Demas,
Send greetings. *(They're here in Rome).[249]
4:15 Greet the Laodicean brothers,
Nympha, and the church in her home.

4:16 When this letter is read to you,
Send it to be read, *I plead,
In the Laodicean church.
Then the letter from there you read.

4:17 Pass this along to Archippus:
"On your service focus your will
Which you received in the Lord
So that it, you might fulfill."

4:18 The greeting that is written here
Is by my own hand, Paul.
Remember my imprisonment.
Grace is truly with you all![250]

THE POETIC FIRST LETTER TO THE THESSALONIANS

1:1 From Paul, Silas, and Timothy,
To the church in Christ the Lord
Among the Thessalonians.
Grace and peace on you are poured.[251]

Your church is in God the Father
And in Jesus Christ the Lord.
1:2 We always thank God for you all
As in our memories, you're stored.

We mention you in our prayer times,
1:3 Recalling your labor of love,
Your work of faith, and your patience
Produced by hope *from above.

In our Lord Jesus the Christ,
Who is *now seated before
The presence of God our Father,
Your hope is fixed *evermore.

1:4 Brothers, you who are loved by God,
We're thanking Him since we know
You are truly chosen ◆by Him.
Election He did bestow.◆

1:5 For our gospel came not to you
In just a verbal depiction.
It came in the Holy Spirit,
In power and much conviction.

Just as[252] we know your election,
You know ours *without mistake.
You know what kind of traits we showed
While laboring* for your sake.

1:6 We who preached and the Lord Himself
Became your imitation
As you received the word with joy
While in much tribulation.

This joy came from the Holy Spirit.
1:7 So, an example you became
To Macedonians and Achaians
Who are believers *in Christ's name.

1:8 For from you the word of the Lord
Has been sounding with a blare,
Not just in Macedonia
Or Achaia, but ◆everywhere.

In every place your faith toward God
Has been traveling around.
So then, there is no need at all
To say anything, we've found.

1:9 For they keep reporting of us
The kind of entrance we gained
When we came into your presence
With the gospel we proclaimed.*

How you turned to God from idols,
Before whom you used to kneel,*
In order to serve the one God,
He who is living and real.

1:10 And to await His Son from heaven
Whom He raised up from the dead,
Jesus who delivers us all
From the wrath coming ahead.

2:1 For you, brothers, know our visit
Has not become without fruit.
2:2 You know before in Philippi
That us they did persecute.

But although we were mistreated
And suffered in that mission,
In faith we preached our God's gospel
To you in much opposition.

2:3 For the urging we made to you
Was not from a wrong perception,
Neither out of impure motives,
Nor by way of deception.

2:4 But just as God has approved to put
The gospel into our care,
To please God who approves our hearts
And not to please men we share.

2:5 For, as you know, we did not come
With flattery to declare,
Neither in a pretense for greed.
God is our witness. ◆I swear!

2:6 We never sought glory from men,
Neither from you nor others,
Though we could have been insistent
As Christ's apostles, *brothers.

2:7 Instead, we became in your midst
As infants,[253] *not overbearing,
Or as if a nursing mother
Were for her children caring.

2:8 Since in this way we longed for you,
Being loved by us with care,
Both God's gospel and our own lives
With you, we were pleased to share.

2:9 For you, brothers, remember that
In hardship, we labored away.
We proclaimed God's gospel to you
While working both night and day.

We did this so on anyone
No burden would be exacted.
2:10 Both you and God are witnesses
As to how we all had acted.◆

How holy, righteous, and blameless
We were to you who believe.
2:11 How we treated each one of you,
Of which you are not naïve.

As a father would his children
2:12 Encourage, console, and urge,
So we kept doing this to you
That this lifestyle would emerge:

Walking in a way that reflects
God's worth *that's beyond compare,
God who calls you into His own
Kingdom and glory *to share.

2:13 And we also always thank God
For how you received God's word
As reported by us to you.
You welcomed all that you heard.

Not as man's word but as is true,
As God's word you did receive,
Which word is also being worked
In all of you who believe.

2:14 For of these churches of God in Christ[254]
You became imitators:
The ones which are in Judea
Who suffered from agitators.

For you suffered in the same things
By your very own countrymen,
Just as they suffered by the Jews
2:15 Who killed the Lord Jesus *back then.

These Jews also killed the prophets,
And us they did persecute.
They don't please God, but toward all men
Are hostile in their pursuit.

2:16 For they work at hindering us
From speaking to the Gentiles
For the purpose that these be saved.
So their sins they heap in piles.◆

Yes, they are always heaping up
Their sins to the highest height,
But upon them, the wrath has come
For the end *not yet in sight.[255]

2:17 Now since we were orphaned from you
A short time, in face, not heart,
We endeavored to see your face
With much longing on our part.

2:18 Because of this we wished to come
Into your presence – I, Paul,
Attempted to come more than once –
Yet Satan hindered us all.

2:19 For who is our hope, or our joy,
Or our victory wreath of pride?
Is it not even you yourselves,
This wreath that will be supplied?*

Before our Lord Jesus's face
When He arrives in full view,
We will receive our victory wreath,*
2:20 For our glory and joy are you.

3:1 So then, no longer bearing it,
We thought it was best to be
Left behind in Athens alone.
3:2 So, we sent you Timothy.

He's our brother, God's coworker
In Christ's gospel, *its report.
We sent him to establish you
And in your faith to exhort.

3:3 This way no one should be shaken
In these tribulations they see,
For you yourselves know very well
That this is our destiny.

3:4 For even when we were with you,
We forewarned you with the word
That we were soon to be afflicted,
Which you know also occurred.

3:5 Because of this tribulation,
Bearing with suspense no more,
I sent to become familiar
With your faithfulness, therefore.

I was thinking that in some way
You the tempter enticed,
And our labor had become vain,
The labor we did for Christ.*

3:6 But Timothy has come to us
Just now from you and has told
The good news of your faith to us
And the selfless love you hold.

He has told us that you possess
Good memories of us always,
Yearning to see us even as
Upon you, we yearn to gaze.

3:7 Because of this report, brothers,
Over you we were consoled
In all our distress and pressure
Through the faithfulness you hold.

3:8 For now we live on, *no more tied
To the unknown of your past,*
Since we now can assume as fact[256]
In the Lord, you're standing fast.

3:9 How can we pay God thanks for you
For all the joy that we shout
In God's presence because of you?
It's inadequate, no doubt.*

3:10 Although, we still pray earnestly.
Both night and day we've pleaded
To see your face and to supply
Your faith with what is needed.

3:11 Now may He, our God and Father,
And Jesus who is our Lord,
Direct our way to your presence.
This wish our prayers record.*

3:12 May the Lord cause your love to grow
And cause it to overflow
For one another and for all
As we do for you also.

3:13 This, then, will establish your hearts
As blameless, ◆without any taints,
With holiness in God's[257] presence
When comes Jesus[258] with all His saints.

4:1 Therefore, brothers, as to what's left,
In the Lord Jesus we plead,
Urging you to progress much more
As we told you to proceed.

You received from us instruction
As to the way in which you ought
To live life so as to please God,
And you're living as we taught.

4:2 For you know what commands we gave
Through the Lord Jesus to you.
4:3 For this, your sanctification,[259]
Is God's will *in all you do.

From all acts of fornication
God wills for you to abstain.
4:4 He wills for each of you to know
How property you must gain.[260]

Acquire it in holiness
And in an honorable way,
4:5 Unlike Gentiles who don't know of God,
Driven by craving *each day.

4:6 God wants each to deal with his brother
So as not to wrong or cheat,
For the Lord as the enforcer
Makes business matters complete.

He will hold you accountable*
As we warned you and said before,
4:7 For God called us in holiness,
Not for uncleanness *to adore.

4:8 So then, he who rejects these things
Does not reject man solely,
But rejects God who gives to you
His Spirit who is holy.

4:9 Now concerning brotherly love,
To write you, you have no need,
For you're taught by God so you love
One another indeed.

4:10 For in all Macedonia
Toward all brothers, you show it.
But we are urging you, brothers,
That even more, you bestow it.

4:11 We urge that you fondly aspire
All offensiveness to shirk,
That is, to mind your own business,
Putting your own hands to work.

We instructed you on these things
4:12 So that decency be your deed
Toward those who are outside *the church,
And so that you aren't in need.

4:13 Now we don't wish for you, brothers,
To be unaware with respect
To those who are asleep *in death
So that *this you might not elect:

That you not grieve as others do,
That is, the rest of the world
Who do not possess any hope
When into death one is hurled.*

4:14 Since we believe that Jesus died
And rose up *not to be kept,
Thus God will also bring with Him
Those who through Jesus have slept.

4:15 For we tell you by the Lord's word
That if we're alive *indeed
Until the coming of the Lord,
Those asleep we won't precede.

4:16 For the Lord Himself will descend
From heaven by a loud broadcast
In a voice of an archangel,
Signaled by God's trumpet blast.

The dead in Christ will be raised first.
4:17 Then we who did not die[261]
Will be snatched with them in the clouds
To meet the Lord in the sky.

Thus we will be with the Lord
Always, •forevermore.
4:18 Keep comforting one another
In these words of hope, therefore.[262]

5:1 As to the times and the seasons
In which these events may fall,[263]
You do not have a need, brothers,
To be written to at all.

5:2 For you yourselves know this full well:
The day of the Lord will arrive
The same way as a thief at night
On unbelievers yet alive.[264]

5:3 When they're saying, "Peace and safety,"
Their swift ruin will come about
Like a pregnant one's labor pains,
And they will have no way out.

5:4 But you yourselves, my dear brothers,
Are not in darkness *but light
So that the day overtake you
As a thief *coming at night.

5:5 For all of you are sons of light,
Sons characterized by day.
We aren't characterized by night.
We're not sons of darkness, *I say.

5:6 So then, let us not be sleeping
Like all those who don't believe,[265]
But let us stay on the alert.
To soberness let us cleave.

5:7 For the practice of those who sleep,
Is to sleep when it is night;
The practice of those who get drunk,
Is to get drunk when it's not light.[266]

5:8 Since we all, *who are believers,
Are characterized by day,
Then let us all conduct ourselves
With soberness in this way:

Wear the breastplate of faith and love.
Put it on once and for all,[267]
And put on the helmet of hope
Which hopes in salvation's call.

5:9 For God did not reserve for us
Wrath as our destination
But through our Lord, Jesus the Christ,
The obtaining of salvation.

5:10 Christ died for us in order that,
When He comes again for our sake,*
We might live together with Him
Whether we're asleep or awake.

5:11 Because of all that has been said,
Keep consoling one another,
And just as you are practicing,
Let one build up the other.

5:12 Brothers, we ask you to acknowledge
Those among you who work hard,
Who also lead you in the Lord
And warn you *as a safeguard.

5:13 We ask that because of their work,
You give them loving respect,
And keep the peace among yourselves.
Unity you must elect.*

5:14 Brothers, we're encouraging you
To warn the unruly sort.
Keep consoling the discouraged.
The spiritually weak, support.

Demonstrate patience before all.
5:15 See to it that no one succeed
In getting even with someone
Because of an evil deed.

Instead, always stay in pursuit
Of that which is good ◆and right
To benefit one another
And all people *in your sight.

5:16 Remain joyful forevermore.
5:17 Continuous prayer pursue.
5:18 In everything keep giving thanks.
God wills this in Christ[268] for you.

5:19 Don't extinguish the Spirit's flame.
5:20 Prophecies never despise,
5:21 But put everything to the test
So God's word you recognize.*

Keep holding on to what is good.
5:22 Make certain that you abstain
From everything that might appear
As if evil you entertain.

5:23 Now may the God of peace Himself
Sanctify you as one whole.
May these be kept as one unit,
Your spirit, body, and soul.

At our Lord Jesus Christ's coming
May they be kept without blame.
5:24 Faithful is the One who calls you,
Who this for you will attain.

5:25 Brothers, keep on praying for us.
5:26 Greet all the brothers like this:
With a greeting that's set apart;[269]
Greet all with a holy kiss.

5:27 I charge you by the Lord to read
This letter to all the others.[270]
5:28 The grace of the Lord Jesus Christ
Is with you all,[271] *my brothers.

THE POETIC SECOND LETTER TO THE THESSALONIANS

1:1 To the Thessalonian church
In God, Father of us all,
Also in the Lord Jesus Christ.
From Timothy, Silas, and Paul.[272]

1:2 To all of you we write these words:*
Grace and peace on you are poured,[273]
Which proceed from God our Father
And from Jesus Christ the Lord.

1:3 To offer thanks to God for you,
Brothers, we're always owing
As is fitting because your faith
Is abundantly growing.

It is fitting because your love
Which each of you pours out
To benefit* one another
Is increasing more, *no doubt.

1:4 So we boast among God's churches
Of your patience and faithfulness
In all of the tribulations
Which you endure *with success.

1:5 This shows God's judgment is righteous
So you might be deemed ◆of worth,
Worthy of the kingdom of God
For which you suffer *on earth.

1:6 For truly it's righteous for God
To repay with tribulation
Those who keep on troubling you,
1:7 And to give you relaxation.

With us, you, the persecuted,
Will rest at the revelation
Of the Lord Jesus from heaven
With this *congregation:

With His mighty angels, He'll come
1:8 In flaming fire to impose
Vengeance on those who know not God
And on those ◆who Him oppose.

To our Lord Jesus's gospel
These are in opposition.
1:9 Both groups will pay the penalty
Of eternal perdition.

Yes, they will pay the penalty
Separated from the Lord's face
And from the glory of His strength
1:10 When He comes *from heaven's place.

He will come to be glorified
In His saints in that day too
And to be the object of awe
Among all believers. *That's you.

For the testimony we gave
Was believed by you also.
1:11 We always pray this prayer for you,
Which we record for you to know:*

That our God might deem you worthy
Of His calling and fulfill
The work of your faith in power
And every good thing you will.

1:12 This way our Lord Jesus's name
Might be glorified in you
And you in Him by our God's grace
And the Lord Jesus Christ's too.

2:1 Now concerning the arrival
Of Jesus Christ our Lord
And our gathering together
Around Him *in one accord.

2:2 We're requesting from you, brothers,
Not to be quickly shaken
Nor to be continually disturbed
In your mind *and be mistaken.

Don't be misled by a spirit,
Or by a word that is taught,
Or by an epistle written
As if from us *but is not.

For there is in circulation
A false claim that has been made
That the day of the Lord has come.
2:3 Don't be so easily swayed.

For the day of the Lord can't come
'Til the apostasy[274] comes first,
And the lawless man is revealed,
The son of ruin, ◆the accursed.

2:4 He stands opposed and exalts himself
Against everything called God,
Or every object of worship
That anyone might have awed.*

He'll sit in God's sanctuary,
Himself as God displaying.
2:5 Don't you recall while still with you
These things to you I was saying?

2:6 You now know the restraining power
Which restrains for the reason
That the lawless man be revealed
In his peculiar season.

2:7 For the mystery of lawlessness
Is working this very day,
But just until the Restrainer[275]
Gets Himself out of the way.

2:8 The lawless one will then be revealed
Whom the Lord will take away[276]
By His mouth's breath, ending that power
When He comes and appears that day.

2:9 The coming of the lawless one,
With Satan's work it complies
In all power, signs, and wonders
That are not true* but are lies.

2:10 His coming is in all deceit
Of unrighteous ambition
For the ones who are on their way
To eternal perdition.

For they did not receive the love
The truth to them did extend
So that they themselves could be saved
From that destructive end.*

2:11 Because of this God will send them
A power that does deceive
With the result that the falsehood
Is what they themselves believe.

2:12 God sends them this in order that
All who did not trust what's true
But enjoyed their unrighteousness
Would receive the judgment due.

2:13 For you, brothers, loved by the Lord,
It is our obligation
To always thank God since He chose you
As first fruits for salvation.[277]

He chose you in connection with
The spirit's sanctification[278]
And with faith in the gospel truth,
The gospel of salvation.◆

2:14 He called you into salvation
Through the gospel which we bring
So as to obtain the glory
Of our Lord Jesus the King.[279]

2:15 So then, brothers, keep standing firm.
Hold on to the things passed down
Taught either through a word from us
Or our letter sent around.

2:16 May our Lord,[280] and God our Father,
Who loved us and to us gave
Eternal comfort and good hope
In the gift of grace that does save -

2:17 May our Lord, and God our Father,
Encourage your hearts *each day
And strengthen you in every deed
And every good word you say.

3:1 Lastly, brothers, keep praying for us
That the word of the Lord would run
And be glorified *by observers
Just as with you this was done.

3:2 Pray that we would be saved from men
Who have crooked and evil ways,
For the faith belongs not to all,
3:3 But the Lord in faithfulness stays.

He will both strengthen and guard you
From the evil one's *own hand.
3:4 We're swayed in the Lord that you do
And will do what we command.

3:5 Now may the Lord direct your hearts
Into the love God displayed
And into the perseverance
Which Christ on earth portrayed.[281]

3:6 Now we're commanding you, brothers,
In the Lord Jesus Christ's name
To stand clear of every brother
Who walks *with a different aim.

Stand clear of the unruly ones
Although they say they believe,*
Yet they don't follow the tradition
Which from us they did receive.

3:7 For you yourselves know very well
How us you must imitate
Because we behaved among you
Without any lazy trait.

3:8 We ate a free meal from no one,
But we worked both night and day
In labor and toil so as not
To burden you in any way.

3:9 We did this not because we lacked
The right to eat a free plate,
But to be a model for you
So that us, you'd imitate.

3:10 For even when we were with you,
This command we did repeat:
"If one is not willing to work,
Then neither should that one eat."

3:11 For we hear that some among you
Walk with a lazy display,
Going around as busybodies
And not working to pay their way.

3:12 Such ones by the Lord Jesus Christ
We order and urge to obey.
By working in orderliness
They must eat their own food *each day.

3:13 But you, brothers, don't grow weary
In doing what is excellent.
3:14 What if someone heeds not our word
Through this letter we will have sent?

Mark this one. Don't mingle with him
So that ashamed he might become.
3:15 Yet don't regard him as a foe,
But as a brother warn this one.

3:16 Now may the Lord of peace Himself
Through every case *big or small
Give you that peace in every way.
The Lord, He is with you all.[282]

3:17 The authentic sign in each letter
Is my handwritten greeting (Paul).
This is the way in which I write.
3:18 Our Lord's[283] grace is with you all.[284]

THE POETIC FIRST LETTER TO TIMOTHY

1:1 Paul, an apostle of Christ Jesus
According to the mandate
Of God our Savior and Christ Jesus,
Our hope *whom we await.

1:2 To Timothy, a true child in faith.
Grace, mercy, and peace *are poured
From God the heavenly Father[285]
And from Jesus Christ our Lord.

1:3 On the way to Macedonia
I encouraged you to stay
In the city of Ephesus
To teach those who went astray.*

Namely, that you instruct them all
To stop teaching heresies
1:4 And to stop holding on to myths
And endless genealogies.

For myths and genealogies
Push conjectures that are flawed
And not what's in the realm of faith,
Our stewardship from God.

1:5 Now the goal of your instruction[286]
Is that selfless love begin
From a clean heart, a good conscience,
And a faith that's genuine.

1:6 From these things, having missed the goal,
Some have strayed into useless speech,
1:7 Wishing to be teachers of law,
Though not mindful ◆of what they teach.

They're not mindful of what they push
Or of their communication,
1:8 But we know that the Law is good
If there is right application.

1:9 We know this: that no law applies
To one who's right *in God's eyes,
But to lawbreakers and rebels
Law most certainly applies.

To ungodly ones and sinners,
To those unholy and profane,
To those who kill their own parents,
To murderers - it does pertain.

1:10 To the sexually immoral,
To those males who with males lie,
To kidnappers, to perjurors,
To liars - it does apply.

Law applies to what opposes
Sound teaching that does accord
1:11 With the blessed God's glorious gospel
Entrusted me *by the Lord.

1:12 I thank our Lord, Jesus the Christ,
The One who empowered me,
Since He considered me faithful
By putting me in ministry.

1:13 I used to be a blasphemer,
A persecutor *well-known,
And a person full of violence,
But mercy to me was shown.

For I did it in unbelief,
Ignorant of any wrong,
1:14 But with faith and love in Jesus[287]
The grace of our Lord flowed strong.

1:15 This message is reliable
And worthy of all approval:
Christ came into the world of sinners
For salvation, *not removal.

I am the greatest of sinners,
1:16 But mercy to me was shown
That in me, the greatest sinner,
Christ Jesus ◆could make this known:

He could show His complete patience
As a pattern *to receive
By those who for eternal life
Would later in Him believe.

1:17 Honor and glory forever
To the King of the ages, then.
He's the immortal, invisible,
And only wise God. Amen.

1:18 This instruction, son Timothy,
Into your hands I now place
As the previous prophecies
Made known concerning your case.

Namely, keep fighting the good fight.
In these prophecies ♦stand your ground
1:19 By always holding on to faith
And to a conscience that is sound.

By rejecting a sound conscience,
This very faith some shipwrecked.
1:20 Hymenaeus and Alexander
Are among those who did reject.

I gave them over to Satan
In order that they might learn
To stop speaking blasphemous words,
And so to the faith return.*

2:1 Therefore, I urge, first and foremost,
That petitions and prayers *combined
With intercessions and thanksgivings
Be poured out for all mankind.

2:2 Keep pouring out prayers for kings
And for all in authority
So we might live calm, peaceful lives
In all godly dignity.

2:3 In the face of our Savior, God,
It's a good and pleasing *show.
2:4 He wants all mankind to be saved
And the truth to come to know.

2:5 For there exists only one God
And one mediator *sufficed
Who is between God and mankind.
He is the Man, Jesus Christ.

2:6 He gave Himself as a ransom
On behalf of all, *not some.
That's the testimony given
As opportunities come.[288]

2:7 As proclaimer and apostle
I was placed to testify,
Teaching Gentiles in faith and truth.
I speak the truth, not a lie.

2:8 Therefore, I decree that the men
Be praying in every place
By lifting hands in holiness.
Wrath and dissension erase.

2:9 Likewise, I decree that women
Adorn themselves in attire
With modesty and decency.
Respectful dress I require.

No braided hairstyles and no gold;
No pearls or expensive clothes;[289]
2:10 Just good works are the proper dress
To claim godliness as the pose.

2:11 In quietness[290] let women learn,
Submissive in every way.
2:12 As for a woman toward a man,
Certain roles she cannot play.*

To take the role of a teacher
Or a leader over a man,
I forbid a woman to do.
Let quietness be her plan.

2:13 For Adam first was formed, then Eve,
And Adam was not deceived,
2:14 But the woman, after being fooled,
To a sinful state, she cleaved.[291]

2:15 Now woman, by bearing children,
Will be saved from trickery[292]
If they remain in faith and love
And holiness with decency.

3:1 Reliable is this saying:
If anybody aspires
To the office of overseer,
A good work he desires.

3:2 Therefore, it is necessary
For every person to meet*
The qualifications listed*
For the overseer's seat:

Above reproach, sober, prudent,
A one-woman kind of man,[293]
Respectable, hospitable,
And to teach God's word he can.

3:3 Not addicted to drinking wine,
Does not with words or hands shove,
But uncontentious and gentle,
And money he does not love.

3:4 A good leader of his household,
Leading his children to subject
Themselves to his authority
With all dignity and respect.

3:5 (But if to lead his own household
A person is not aware,
How can he have abilities
For the church of God to care?)

3:6 He must not be a new convert,
For in pride he might revel.
This way he won't fall into
The judgment of the Devil.

3:7 A good testimony of him
Those outside the church[294] must bear
So that he might not fall into
The shame of the Devil's snare.[295]

3:8 Likewise, deacons *must qualify.
They must be worthy of respect.
They don't engage in double-talk,
And drinking much wine they reject.

They don't pursue dishonest gain.
3:9 The mystery called faith they hold
In the realm of a clean conscience.
As deacons these may be enrolled.*

3:10 However, testing must come first.
Their character you observe.*
If they're blameless •and pass the test,
Then let them as deacons serve.

3:11 Likewise women[296] *must qualify.
They must be worthy of respect,
Not gossipy, but temperate.
All faithfulness they reflect.

3:12 Let deacons, *like overseers,
Be one-woman kind of men,
Good leaders over their households
And over their own children.

3:13 For those who serve well do produce
A standing for themselves that's sound
And much boldness in their faithfulness
Which in Christ Jesus is found.

3:14 These things I am writing to you,
Though I hope to see you with speed.
3:15 If I delay, you now know how
In God's house, these must proceed.

It's the church of the living God,
Truth's pillar and foundation.
3:16 How great is the godly mystery
By common recitation:[297]

"He was manifested in flesh,
Unveiled for the world to see.*
In spirit, He was justified.
Over death He gained victory.*

"He was observed by messengers.[298]
To nations was preached His story.
He was believed among the world.
He was taken up in glory."

4:1 But the Spirit blatantly says
That in later times to come[299]
Some will stand away from the faith
And pursue another one.*

They will heed deceptive spirits
And teachings demons inspire
4:2 In the hypocrisy of men,
Each of them being a liar.

The consciences of these liars
Have been seared by an iron's heat.
4:3 They forbid people to marry,
And list foods they're not to eat.

Yet God created all these foods
To be thankfully received
By those who've come to know the truth,
By those who have believed.

4:4 For all God's creation is good,
And nothing we thankfully share
4:5 Is a waste, for it's sanctified
By the word of God and prayer.

4:6 By teaching the brothers these things,
Jesus Christ's good servant you'll be,
Being nourished in the words of faith,
That good teaching you've come to see.

4:7 Avoid worldly philosophies
Which are merely old wives' tales,
But like an athlete train yourself
So that godliness prevails.

4:8 For there is little benefit
In just bodily training,
But godliness benefits *much.
In all things, you are gaining.

For it holds the promise of life
For the next life and now *on earth.
4:9 This message is reliable.
All approval it is worth.

4:10 Since we've hoped in the living God,
For this,[300] we toil and strain.
He's the Savior of all mankind,
Specially those who trust *His name.

4:11 Keep charging and teaching these things.
4:12 Let none on your youth look down,
But you become an example
To the believers *in that town.

Be an example in your word
And in the way that you live.
In love, in faith, in purity
Yourself as an example give.

4:13 Until I come, pay attention
To the reading *of God's word,
To giving encouragement *from it,
To teaching *it as you've heard.

4:14 Do not neglect the gift in you
Unveiled as part of God's plans*
Through prophecy when the elders
Upon you had laid their hands.

4:15 Attend to these things. In them live
That your progress to all be plain.
4:16 Watch yourself, and watch your teaching.
In them continually remain.

For by practicing all these things,
You will most certainly save
Yourself and those listening to you
From deception demons wave.[301]

5:1 Do not rebuke an older man,
But encourage him instead
As if he were your own father.
Encourage him as I've said.*

Treat younger men as your brothers,
5:2 Older women as your mothers.
As your sisters, treat younger gals.
In all purity treat others.

5:3 Honor widows who are widows
In the truest sense of the word.
5:4 If any widow has children
Or grandchildren, *let this be heard:

Let all her progeny learn first
To be godly in their own home
And repay their progenitors.
God is pleased by this *alone.

5:5 The true widow, bereft of kin,
In God her hope positions.
She continues both day and night
In prayers and petitions.

5:6 But she who lives in luxury,
Although living, she has died.
5:7 Give these orders so that widows
Will have no blame applied.

5:8 If for their own, chiefly in the home,
They decide to not provide,
They are worse than an infidel,
And the faith they have denied.

5:9 Let a widow be registered
Who's not less than sixty years old,
And a one-man kind of woman
In her actions must be told.[302]

5:10 She must testify by good works,
Assuming by these she's been known:
She has brought up her children well;
Hospitality she has shown.

She has washed the feet of the saints;
The troubled she has assisted;
In every kind of work that's good
She has truly persisted.

5:11 Don't provide for younger widows,
For when desires are unburied
Which govern them instead of Christ,
They tend to want to get married.

5:12 They'll be judged since *celibacy,[303]
Their former pledge, they've rejected.
5:13 Besides, they tend to learn idleness,
Visiting homes they've selected.

They don't just tend to be idle,
But tend to gossip a lot.
They tend to be busybodies,
Talking of things they should not.

5:14 So, I direct younger widows
To marry and children produce,
To keep the home and give no place
To the enemy for abuse.

5:15 For already it has occurred
That some young widows have strayed,
To follow after the Devil.[304]
Into Satan's hand, they've played.◆

5:16 If any female believer[305]
Has widows in her own care,
Let her *use her personal means
To help them in their welfare.

Do not let the church be burdened
By needs which can be supplied*
So that it can give assistance
To widows who are qualified.

5:17 Make sure the elders who lead well
Are deemed worthy of double pay,
Especially those who in preaching
And in teaching labor away.

5:18 For the Scripture clearly declares,
"A muzzle on an ox don't lay
While it is treading out the grain."
And "The worker is worth his pay."

5:19 A charge made against an elder
You are not to entertain
Except if the testimony
Of two or three are the same.

5:20 Rebuke in everyone's presence
Those who continue in sin
In order that everyone else
Might be full of fear within.

5:21 Before God, Christ, and chosen angels,
I charge that these things you guard
Without bias and do nothing
Without favoritism barred.

5:22 Lay hands on no one hastily.
Of their qualities be sure.[306]
Don't contribute to others' sins.
Continually keep yourself pure.

5:23 Don't just drink water anymore,
But mix it with a little wine
For the sake of your own stomach
Since you're ill much of the time.

5:24 Some people's sins are obvious,
Leading to judgment of some kind,
But yet as for other people,
Their sins follow far behind.

5:25 So also it is with good works.
Some are immediately plain,
Yet others that are not that way
Concealed they cannot remain.

6:1 All bond slaves under slavery's yoke,
Their masters by them must be deemed
Worthy of honor so God's name
And teaching won't be blasphemed.

6:2 Slaves who have believing masters,
Don't let them show disrespect
Since they are brothers *in the Lord,
But service let them elect.

For they are fellow believers
And dearly loved *in God's eyes,
Devoting themselves to good deeds.
These things you teach and advise.

6:3 If someone teaches differently
Than that of Christ Jesus our Lord,
Not agreeing with sound teaching
That with godliness does accord -

6:4 He's been puffed up, knowing nothing.
He just has a sickly craving
For controversies and disputes
Which leads to *misbehaving.

It leads to envy and to strife,
To evil speculations,
To blasphemies, and between men
6:5 To constant irritations.

I speak of men deprived of the truth
Who have a corrupted brain,
Who think godliness is to be
A means of personal gain.

6:6 But godliness with contentment
Is a means of gain, *no doubt,
6:7 For we brought nothing into this world,
And we can take nothing out.

6:8 Since we have food and covering,
With these, we must be content,
6:9 But those who fixate on being rich
On a trap make their descent.

They fall to foolish and harmful lusts
Set by the trap of temptation
Which plunges people deep into
Destruction and devastation.

6:10 For setting your adoration
On anything monetary
Is a root that leads to evil
Of kinds that widely vary.

Some by it have strayed from the faith
As for it they've stretched to pursue.
As a result, with many pains
They have pierced themselves right through.

6:11 But you yourself, O man of God,
From these things keep on fleeing.
Chase right, godly, and faithful things,
Love, patience, and a gentle being.

6:12 Keep fighting the good fight of faith.
Of the eternal life grab hold.
That's the life to which you were called
And into which *you were enrolled.

You confessed the good confession
In many witnesses' sight.
6:13 So, I command you before God
Who to all things, gives life's *light.

I command you before Christ Jesus
Who before Pontius Pilate stood
And testified *in word and deed
The confession that is good.

6:14 Keep the command I gave before
Without blame and without stain
'Til the time our Lord Jesus Christ
Makes His appearance plain.

6:15 In His own time, He'll fulfill it,
The sole ruler and the blessed.
He's King of kings and Lord of lords.
He's different from all the rest.[307]

6:16 Just He holds immortality,
Lives in light inaccessible.
None of humanity saw Him.
To see Him is impossible.

This affords a doxology*
Which I record with a pen:*
To Him, honor *unparalleled
And eternal power. Amen.

6:17 Charge the present day wealthy ones
Not to live in pride's scope.
On the uncertainty of wealth,
Charge them not to fix their hope.

6:18 Instead, charge them to fix their hope
On God who lavishly supplies
All things to us for enjoyment.
Security in Him lies.*

Charge them to keep on doing good,
And in good works to be rich.
Charge them to be generous
And that sharing *be their niche.

6:19 This way they're storing for themselves
For the age that's yet to be
A good foundation so as to grasp
What's life in reality.

6:20 Guard the deposit, Timothy,
By turning from godless chatter
And from all the contradictions
Of the pseudo knowledge matter.[308]

6:21 Some have set up a profession[309]
By this knowledge they declare
And so they have strayed from the faith.
Grace is with all of you there![310]

THE POETIC SECOND LETTER TO TIMOTHY

1:1 Paul, apostle of Jesus Christ
By God's will and in accord
To the promise about the life
In Jesus Christ *the Lord:

1:2 To Timothy, dearly loved child.
Grace, mercy, and peace are poured[311]
Upon you from God the Father
And from Jesus Christ our Lord.

1:3 I possess gratitude toward God
Who's rich in my ancestry,
Whom I serve with a clear conscience,
For you're in my memory.

I constantly remember you
In my prayers both night and day,
1:4 Longing to see you and be joyful,
For your tears in my mind replay.

1:5 I thank God because I've received
A reminder of what's in you,
A faith without hypocrisy
Which dwelled in your *ancestry too.

First in your grandmother Lois,
In your mother Eunice as well,
And I am fully persuaded
That in you it too does dwell.

1:6 For this reason, I remind you
That you keep the fire fanned,
Stirring God's gift you have within
Through the laying on of my hand.

1:7 For God, He did not give to us
A spirit that makes us cower
But one of love, and self-control,
And one described by power.

1:8 Therefore, do not allow yourself
To have a spirit of shame[312]
Of the witness about our Lord
Or of me, chained for His *name.

Suffer with me in the gospel
According to God's power.
1:9 He saved and called us to a calling
That's holy. *So, don't cower.

He did not save us and call us
By our works *(they're not sufficed)
But by His own plan that grace would be
Given us in Jesus Christ.

Before the times of the ages
His plan of grace was sealed,[313]
1:10 But through our Savior's appearance
That grace has now been revealed.

For Jesus Christ abolished death,
And into the light He brought
Both life and immortality
Through the gospel *that's now taught.

1:11 As for this gospel, I myself
Was appointed as a preacher,
As an apostle *to the world,
And also as a teacher.

1:12 Because of my service to Christ
In the gospel, I've proclaimed,
These things I now am suffering,
But I'm in no way ashamed.

I know in whom I have trusted,
And my confidence is firm:
He's able to guard my deposit
For that day *of His return.

1:13 To the standard of those sound words
Which you heard from me, so cling
In faith and sacrificial love
Which is in Jesus the King.[314]

1:14 Guard that good deposit I made,
The sound words you did receive.◆
Guard it through the Holy Spirit
Who dwells in us *who believe.

1:15 All in Asia were turned from me
As you already well know.
Phygelus and Hermogenes
Are among those who did go.

1:16 May God[315] grant mercy to this one's home,
Onesiphorus is his name,
Since many times he refreshed me
And was not ashamed of my chain.

1:17 But as soon as he came to Rome,
With diligence, he did seek
Until he finally found me.
So, this blessing I now speak:*

1:18 May the Lord grant that on that day
He finds mercy from the Lord.
How often he served in Ephesus,
You know well *and haven't ignored.

2:1 Therefore, my child, keep empowered
In the grace which in Christ[316] is found.
2:2 All the things which you heard from me
Many witnesses resound.[317]

Entrust those things to faithful men
Because *the workers will swell.
That many more will be able
To teach other people as well.

2:3 As I suffer in serving Christ,*
Suffer with me, *as you should,
As a soldier of Jesus Christ,
Who is excellent◆ and good.

2:4 No one serving as a soldier
Is entangled in life's affairs
So that pleasing his commander
Be the focus of his cares.

2:5 Also, in an athletic match
There's never to be an athlete
Who receives a victory crown
That unlawfully does compete.

2:6 The farmer who is diligent
(An essential attribute,◆
A primary necessity)[318]
Shares in the various fruit.

2:7 Keep going over in your mind
Everything that I have penned,[319]
For the Lord in everything
Will help you to comprehend.

2:8 Keep remembering Jesus Christ
As now risen from the dead,
A descendant◆ of David's seed,
Matching the gospel I spread.

2:9 In which I'm suffering badly
To the extent that I am found
To be chained as a criminal,
But God's word has not been bound.

2:10 Therefore, all things I do endure
For the chosen people's sake
So that the salvation in Christ
With eternal glory they take.

2:11 This message is reliable,
Which to you I now will give:*
If we truly have died with Him,
With Him, we will also live.

2:12 If we continue enduring,
With Him we will also reign;
That One will surely deny us
If we will deny His name.[320]

2:13 If we are unfaithful to Him,
Faithful that One will remain,
For it's not even possible
For Him to deny His name.[321]

2:14 Keep reminding them of these things
As you warn them in God's sight
(That's to say the people of faith)*
That over words they not fight.

For fighting over words results
In nothing of any use.
Those who hear the fight over words,
Their ruin this can produce.

2:15 Work hard to show yourself to God
As approved *and undeterred,
As a worker who's unashamed
By rightly handling truth's word.

2:16 Avoid worldly and empty talk,
For those doing this routine
End up in more ungodliness.
2:17 Their talk will spread like gangrene.

Hymenaeus and Philetus
Are among those *we've observed
2:18 Who engage in this kind of talk,*
Who around the truth have swerved.

They're upsetting some people's faith
By saying to everyone
That the final resurrection
Through faith[322] has already come.

2:19 Nevertheless, God's foundation
Is firm and remains to stand
With the following inscription
Stamped *by the Lord's own hand:

"The Lord knows[323] in a personal way
All those who to Him belong.
All who name the name of the Lord
Depart from all that is wrong."

2:20 In a large house there are vessels,
Each made in a certain way.◆
Some are made of silver and gold,
But others of wood and clay.

All the vessels have their own use,◆
Some for honorable events.
Others have no honor at all,
Used in an everyday sense.*

2:21 Therefore, if one cleans himself up,
Ridding himself of all sin,[324]
That one will be a vessel used
For honored reasons by Him.

That person will be set apart,
For the Master's use *as declared,
And for every kind of good work
So that he'll be fully prepared.

2:22 Keep running from all those desires
That pertain to youthful lust,
But keep running after those things
That pertain to godly trust.*

Keep running after righteousness,
Faith, peace and unselfish love.
Run with those who from a clean heart
Call upon the Lord *above.

2:23 Keep avoiding all those disputes
Of the foolish and untrained,
Because you know what they produce,
Conflict *that is unrestrained.

2:24 The Lord's servant must never be
One who is full of quarrels
But one who is to everyone
Full of the following morals:*

Gentle and tolerant when wronged;
Skilled in teaching *his mission;
2:25 Gently correcting those who place
Themselves in opposition.

As you conduct yourself this way,
Perhaps God might to them give
A repentance that leads into
Knowing the truth *and so live.

2:26 They might see the reality
And escape from the Devil's snare,
Being captured alive by God
To do His will *and not err.[325]

3:1 Keep learning that in the last days
Difficult times will arrive,
3:2 For mankind will become as those
Who in these qualities strive:*

Infatuated with one's self;
Giving money adoration;
Always bragging and showing off;
Full of evil conversation.

Disobedient to parents;
Unthankful and without heart;
3:3 Unwilling to keep any peace;
In gossip taking part.

Unholy, reckless, and hostile;
Traitors and haters of good;
3:4 Thoughtless, prideful, adoring pleasure
Instead of God *as they should.

3:5 They hold on to an outward form
Of godliness, *as they'd say,
Yet completely deny its power.
From these people turn away.

3:6 For some of them sneak into homes
And work hard to captivate
Weak women led by many lusts
Under sin piles of great weight.

3:7 These women are always learning.
Yet no power can they possess
To come into the full knowledge
Of the truth *which we express.

3:8 Even as Jannes and Jambres[326]
Opposed Moses beforehand,
So too, those who sneak into homes
Against the truth firmly stand.

They're men whose minds have been depraved.
As to faith, they've failed the test,
But though they persist in their deeds,*
3:9 Their progress will be suppressed.

For their lack of understanding
To everyone will become clear
As the magicians' ignorance[327]
Eventually did appear.

3:10 But you have investigated
My teaching and the way I live,
My purpose, faith, and endurance,
And love which I selflessly give.

3:11 Yes, you have investigated*
The perseverance I hold,
The persecutions and sufferings
Which upon me did unfold.

The persecutions I endured
In Antioch *you recall,
In Iconium and Lystra too.
The Lord rescued me from all.

3:12 Anyone who truly wishes
(It's a fact that's undisputed)*
To live godly in Christ Jesus
Will surely be persecuted.

3:13 Evil men and those who swindle
Will progressively get worse
As they keep on being deceived,
And their deception they disperse.

3:14 But you keep living in the things
Which you learned and have believed,
Since you personally know from whom
You learned them *and received.

3:15 For from your childhood you have known
The Scriptures[328] which can make you wise
To place your faith in Christ Jesus
So that salvation He supplies.

3:16 Every Scripture is God-inspired
And is beneficial *no less
For teaching, rebuke, correction,
And training in righteousness.

3:17 This way the man of God can be
Adequately qualified,
Fully equipped for every kind
Of good work to be applied.

4:1 Before our God and Christ Jesus
Who'll judge the dead and the living,
And by His appearance and kingdom,
This charge to you I'm giving:

4:2 Proclaim the word and be ready
In both good times and in sour.
Rebuke, convict, and encourage
As you teach in patient *power.

4:3 For time will come when sound teaching
They won't endure, but they'll hoard
Teachers who scratch their itching ears,
Feeding the desires they've stored.

4:4 They'll turn their hearing from the truth.
As to myths, their ears will perk,
4:5 But you keep sober in all things.
Bear hardships. Do gospel work.

Completely fulfill your service,
4:6 For already I've been contrived
As a drink offering that's poured out.
My departure time has arrived.

4:7 I have struggled the good struggle.
The course I have completed.
I have remained in faithfulness.
4:8 As a victor I'll be seated.◆

The victor's crown of righteousness
For me is being stored away
Which the Lord, the righteous judge,
Will give me in that day.

Yet not just me but everyone
Who has loved His appearance,
He will give this victory crown.
We've run with perseverance.*

4:9 Visit me as soon as you can
With diligence asserted,
4:10 For Demas loves this present age,
And me he has deserted.

He went to Thessalonica.
Crescens went to Galatia.
Luke is the only one with me.
Titus went to Dalmatia.

4:11 Go and get Mark. Bring him with you.
His ministry I can use.
4:12 Tychicus went to Ephesus,
But this for him I did choose.

4:13 My cloak is with Carpus in Troas.
When you come bring it with you.
And bring the scrolls, especially
The parchments *for me to view.

4:14 Alexander the coppersmith
Much evil to me has shown.
This man the Lord will recompense
According to the works he's sown.

4:15 Against Alexander, you too,
Be constantly on your guard,
For all our words which we proclaim
He stood against strong ◆and hard.

4:16 At my trial,◆ my first defense,
To stand with me no one sought.
But everyone abandoned me.
May against them, no charge be brought.

4:17 The Lord stood by me, strengthened me,
So that through me He might cause
The message for all Gentiles to hear.
I was saved from the lions' jaws.

4:18 The Lord will from all evil work
Rescue me *again and again
For His own heavenly kingdom.
Endless glory to Him! Amen.

4:19 Onesiphorus's household
And Prisca and Aquila, greet.
4:20 Erastus remained in Corinth.
City treasurer is his seat.[329]

But Trophimus I had to leave
In Miletus since he was ill.
4:21 Come visit me before winter.
With diligence please fulfill.

Eubulus sends you his greetings,
Also Pudens and Linus do.
Claudia and all the brothers
Send their greetings to you.

4:22 The Lord is with *you, Timothy,
With your spirit, *I declare.
The undeserved free gift called* grace
Is with you believers there.[330]

THE POETIC LETTER TO TITUS

1:1 From Paul, a bond slave serving God
And Christ's[331] apostle *sent out
To bring to faith those whom God chose
And to spread truth's knowledge about.

This is a full and real knowledge,[332]
Which to godliness does comply,
1:2 Based on hope in eternal life
Which God promised, and He can't lie.

Before the times of the ages
He had this promise in place,
1:3 But made His word known in His time
In the preaching *of this grace.

I was entrusted with this word
To proclaim the promised favor
In accordance with the command
Of God who is our Savior.

1:4 To Titus, a genuine child
By a common faith *sufficed.
Grace and peace from God the Father
And our Savior Jesus Christ.

1:5 I left you in Crete for this cause:
That what remains, you set right,
Placing elders in each city
Just as you, I did incite.

1:6 Anyone placed must be blameless,
A one-woman man, *truly,[333]
With faithful children[334] not accused
Of being wild or unruly.

1:7 For it is a necessity
That as a steward of God
An overseer be blameless,
With character to applaud.◆

He's not self-willed or quick-tempered.
From drunkenness, he does abstain.
He is not a man of violence,
And does not seek shady gain.

1:8 However, he's hospitable.
He is fond of all that's good.
He's prudent, righteous, self-controlled,
And lives like a true saint should.[335]

1:9 He holds firm to the faithful word,
As the teaching does disclose,
So he can exhort with sound teaching
And reprove those who oppose.

1:10 For there are many who are rebels,
And make nonsense their decision,
And there are many deceivers,
Mostly from the circumcision.

1:11 It's essential to silence them
Since whole households they upset,
Teaching what's not necessary
For dishonest gain to get.

1:12 As one of their own prophets said,
"Cretans, they always lie.
They're evil beasts and lazy gluttons."
1:13 The truth he did testify.

For this reason, rebuke them all
With sharpness concerning their wrong
In order that they in the faith
May become healthy ◆and strong.

1:14 Make sure they stop giving their ears
To Jewish myths *to be learned
And to the commandments of men
Who are from the truth being turned.

1:15 To those who are spiritually clean,[336]
Everything is clean as well.
To the defiled, nothing is clean
Since no faith in them does dwell.[337]

But both their thinking and conscience
Has been defiled, ◆full of stain!
1:16 They profess to know about God,
But they really deny *His name.

For by their works they deny Him.
Detestable *they have stood.
They're rebellious and unapproved
For every work that is good.

2:1 But you yourself keep on speaking
The things that truly befit
Teaching that is healthy ♦and strong.
To the following teach it:*

2:2 Older men are to be sober,
In dignity and prudence found.
In faith, in love, and in patience
They are to be very sound.

2:3 Older women must be, likewise,
Respectful in every way,
Not enslaved by excessive wine,
Not slanderous in what they say.

They must be teachers of what's good
2:4 In order that they may *suffice
As those qualified in giving
Younger women their advice.

To the women that are younger,
Let the older women tell
To show affection to their husbands
And to their children as well.

2:5 To be prudent, good homemakers,
In all holiness *immersed,
Submissive to their own husbands
So God's word might not be cursed.

2:6 Likewise, encourage younger men
To be prudent, *as all should,
2:7 Showing yourself in every way
As a model of doing good.

In your teaching show purity.
Show dignity as you teach.
2:8 Make sure* it is beyond reproach.
I'm referring to* sound speech.

This way one of opposition
May be turned by feeling shame,
Having nothing terrible at all
About us that he can claim.

2:9 Slaves are to be in subjection
To their masters in every way.
They are not to be talking back
But well-pleasing *as they obey.

2:10 To be completely faithful and good
They must prove (steal, they must not)
So that they may in every way
Adorn what our Savior[338] has taught.

2:11 For the salvific grace of God
Has appeared for all mankind,
2:12 Training us in this present age
To live *in a way that's refined.

Ungodliness and worldly lusts,
Grace keeps training us to deny.
Prudent, righteous, and godly ways,
It keeps training us to apply.

2:13 Thus we live in this present age
As the blessed hope, we await,
Jesus Christ's appearance in glory,[339]
Our God and Savior who's great.

2:14 He gave Himself on our behalf
So that us He might redeem,
Freeing* us from all lawlessness,
From sin's tyrannical regime.[340]

He gave Himself on our behalf
So as for Himself to make pure
A chosen people full of zeal
For good works to secure.

2:15 Keep speaking, urging, rebuking
With all authority in view,
And do not allow anyone
To ever look down upon you.

3:1 Keep reminding them all, *Titus,
That to those in authority,
To rulers in the government,
That submissive they must be.

Keep telling them to be prepared
For every kind of good deed,
3:2 To speak evil of nobody,
In quarrels not to proceed.

Keep telling them to be gentle,
And that they show courtesy
To all mankind, ◆to all people,
Regardless of who they may be.*

3:3 For we ourselves were once foolish,
Faithless, being led astray,
Serving many lusts and pleasures,
Living in evil each day.*

We were once living in envy,
Despicable, living in hate,
Just despising one another.
We lived in a sinful state.*

3:4 But when God our Savior's kindness,
His fondness for man, ◆His care,
Became visible *to our eyes,
He saved us *right then and there.

3:5 He saved us not by righteous works
Which we had deemed as worth,[341]
But according to His mercy
Through the washing of rebirth.

He saved us by the renewal
Which the Holy Spirit did bring
3:6 Whom He richly poured out on us
Through Our Savior Jesus the King.[342]

3:7 He saved us so we could be heirs
And so hope in life eternal,
Being declared righteous by the grace
Of that One *who is supernal.

3:8 The message is reliable,
And concerning these things, then,
I intend for you to assert
Over and over again.

This way they who have trusted God
Might be focused as they should
On their devotion to good works.
These are useful to man's good.

3:9 Keep avoiding foolish disputes,
Genealogies and strife,
And quarrels over Jewish law.
They're useless, empty *of life.

3:10 Reject a divisive person
After warnings issued twice,
3:11 Knowing such one is warped and sins.
He's self-condemned *by this vice.

3:12 When Artemas or Tychicus
I send to you *there in Crete,
Work to come to Nicopolis
So that you and I can meet.

For I have made the decision
To spend the whole winter there.
3:13 Zenas the lawyer and Apollos,
Send them with the greatest care.

Do so in order to ensure
That they have all that they need.
Seek the help of believers there
In fulfilling this good deed.[343]

3:14 Let our fellow believers learn
Good works must be their pursuit,
Meeting pressing needs *like this
So they won't be without fruit.

3:15 All those with me send you greetings.
Greet those whose affections fall
On you and me in faithfulness.
Grace is present with you all.[344]

THE POETIC LETTER TO PHILEMON

1:1 From Paul, in chains for Jesus Christ,
And from brother Timothy:
To Philemon our coworker,
Loved dearly *by him and me.

1:2 Also to sister Apphia,
To our fellow soldier who's known
By the name of Archippus,
And to the church in your home.

1:3 To all of you I write these words:*
Grace and peace on you are poured,[345]
Which proceed from God our Father
And from Jesus Christ the Lord.

1:4 I always give thanks to my God
As I make mention of you
During the time of my prayers
1:5 Since I hear this *to be true:

Your unselfish love *overflows
As well as the faith you hold
In the face of the Lord Jesus
And toward all the saints, *I'm told.

1:6 I pray the sharing of your faith
Works with power *without mistake
As you experience within you[346]
All that is good for Christ's sake.

1:7 For based upon your selfless love
Much joy and comfort I've got
Since to the saint's hearts, my brother,
Refreshment you have brought.

1:8 Therefore, although having in Christ
Enough boldness to insist
For you to do what is proper,
This stringent tone I resist.*

1:9 Instead, I'm encouraging you
For the sake that love *remains,
Since I, Paul, am such an old man,
Now for Christ Jesus in chains.

1:10 I encourage you with regards
To Onesimus my child
Whom I fathered while in my chains.
I beg you, be reconciled.*

1:11 He used to be useless to you
But *that is no longer true.
He's presently very useful
To not only me but you.

1:12 I am sending him back to you.
That means my heart I send.
1:13 I was planning to keep him here
So that to me he would attend.

That he'd serve me on your behalf
In my chains for the good news,
1:14 But I don't wish to do anything
Without your consent. *I refuse.

This is so that the good you do
Will not be under duress
But ◆according to your choosing,
According to your willingness.

1:15 Perhaps he was separated
For this fairly brief season
That you might have him back forever.
Perhaps this is the reason.

1:16 But not that you receive him back
As your own slave anymore,
But better than that, a brother
On whom our love we outpour.

He's a brother, specially to me,
On whom my love is outpoured,
But how much more he'd be to you
In the flesh and in the Lord.

1:17 Therefore, if as your partner
You consider me to be,
Then I beg you as your partner,*
Receive him as you would me.

1:18 But if he wronged you in some way
Or in some debt, he does stand,
Then charge this to my own account.
1:19 I, Paul, write this by my hand.

I will compensate you myself,
And although you owe me your soul,
I'm not saying that besides this
You're financially in the hole.[347]

1:20 Yes, brother, may I derive joy
In the realm of the Lord from you.
Give my heart refreshment in Christ.
Your obedience is true.

1:21 Having the fullest confidence
That your obedience is true,
I write this knowing you will do
Above what I'm asking of you.

1:22 But at the same time do this too:
Prepare me a place to stay.
I hope to be God's gift[348] to you
Through the prayers that you pray.

1:23 My fellow captive in Christ Jesus,
Epaphras sends greetings to you.
1:24 My coworkers, Aristarchus,
Mark, Demas, and Luke do too.

1:25 The undeserved free gift of* grace
Which from the Lord Jesus Christ came
Is with your[349] spirit *all the time!
This is a fact to exclaim.[350]

ENDNOTES

1 Literally, *His holy prophets.*
2 The word *apostle* literally means, *one sent out.*
3 The Greek text does not reflect a wish, but exclaims a fact.
4 Literally, *all who believe.*
5 Paul quotes Habakkuk 2:4 to support the argument that righteousness can only be attained by faith. Therefore, this quote should not be translated as *the righteous will live by faith.* It should be translated as *the righteous by faith will live.* The idea is that those who are declared righteous by means of their faith are the ones who will live eternally.
6 The Greek word is *amen* which literally means *truly.*
7 The Greek word is *epignosis,* referring to a personal knowledge as opposed to an intellectual knowledge.
8 In the Greek text, there is a distinction between *law* and *Law.* The apostle Paul makes this distinction by inserting or omitting the definite article *the.* English translations often do not reflect this difference. When the apostle wants the reader to know that he is referring to only the Law of Moses, he puts *the* before the word, *law.* If that is the case, *law* will be capitalized. If Paul wants the reader to know that he is referring to law in general, which may or may not include the Mosaic law, he would omit the definite article, *the.* If that is the case, *law* will not be capitalized. In some instances it will be translated as *rule, guide,* or something similar.
9 Derived from 2:28,29.
10 Derived from Deuteronomy 7:25.
11 Derived from Mark 7:8. The Jew kept traditional law even if it violated the Law of Moses.
12 Implied.
13 *By God* is not stated in the Greek text but it is implied.
14 Derived from verse 22.
15 The Greek word was commonly used to refer to a payment that satisfied the anger of the gods.

16 Paul's point is not that Abraham is the father of those physically circumcised, specifically the Jewish race, but he is the spiritual father of the Jew who has the same faith as Abraham.

17 Implied in the next verse.

18 The Greek word for *love* in this verse is *agape* which refers to an unselfish act for the benefit of another's good. The meaning of *agape* will not always be footnoted but will be often translated in this volume as *unselfish love* or something similar.

19 The literal word is *reconciliation* which refers to the restoration of those at odds with each other to peace.

20 Implied.

21 The last two stanzas are derived from verses 6 and 14.

22 Literally, *Christ Jesus.*

23 The Greek tense does not emphasize a lifestyle of sin as it did in the first half of this chapter. The tense speaks of instances of sin. A Christian cannot have the lifestyle of sin, but he does sin from time to time.

24 Literally, *May it not happen.*

25 Bible scholars differ as to whether Paul is narrating his past or his present. In narratives it was not uncommon for the narrator to speak of past events in the present tense. The gospel narratives abound with this (e.g. Mark 3:13,20,31). It is my opinion that Paul is narrating his past life as a religious Jew, having the inability to overcome the lifestyle of coveting at that time. This is consistent with the previous context of being freed from sin to serve God (chapter 6). It is also consistent with the following context of the condition of being in the flesh and therefore not having God's Spirit and not belonging to Christ (7:9). The greater context of the New Testament also supports this understanding (1 Corinthians 6:10; 1 John 3:9,10).

26 Derived from the next verses.

27 Derived from the idea in verse 15.

28 Literally, *in Christ Jesus.*

29 The Greek tense does not emphasize an instance of following the sin nature but a lifestyle.

30 More literally, *by the one who subjected.* This no doubt refers to the curse of God on the earth because of Adam's sin.

31 There is debate over whether to translate this as *what to pray* or *how to pray.* Both ideas are included in this quatrain.

32 The context supports the idea that the wordless groans are ours (verse 23), not the Spirit's.

33 Literally, *foreknew.* The Greek word expresses a personal knowing beforehand, not the knowing of facts. Eternal life is knowing God and His Son in a personal way. See Matthew 7:23 and John 17:3 to understand the meaning of the root form of this word.

34 The word *firstborn* has only two meanings: (1) the first one born in a family, or (2) one who has authority. The second meaning developed out of the ancient custom of the firstborn becoming the head of the family. The latter meaning applies here.

35 Although the act of glorifying is viewed as a past act in the Greek text, it is yet future in reality. This literary technique communicates the absolute certainty of a future event. The future glorification of believers is as good as done.

36 The Greek tense emphasizes an ongoing mediation.

37 The Greek word for *wish* is in the imperfect indicative, which would ordinarily put the wish in the past: *I was wishing*. But Paul is explaining how he feels now: *My grief is heavy*. The ancient Greek language follows this pattern to express an exaggeration that falls short of reality: *I could almost wish*.

38 Literally, *I will have mercy on whom I have mercy, and I will have compassion on whom I have compassion*." The point of saying it this way is that God does not have to have a reason to shower mercy or compassion on a person.

39 Literally, *the Lord of hosts*.

40 The Greek word for *knowledge* emphasizes a personal relationship. See 1:28 notes.

41 Literally, *the abyss*. It is very difficult to understand the point of these quotes from Deuteronomy 30:12-14 with the parenthetic comments of bringing Christ down and raising Him up. The original point of the passage is that God's message of life is not out of reach but has been set before us to trust. The parenthetic thought of Christ coming down from heaven and being raised from death is to show how the gospel message was made plain in Christ – His incarnation and resurrection.

42 Derived from the next verse.

43 Literally, *whom He foreknew*. See 8:29 note.

44 Derived from 1:5.

45 Implied.

46 The rest of the chapter should be seen in connection to the subject of spiritual gifts.

47 The Greek word carries the general idea of continuance. Therefore, it can mean *to persist* or *to devote*.

48 Derived from verse 2.

49 Literally, *God*.

50 Literally, *the wrath*. This is referring to the wrath in the previous verse, the punishment inflicted by government for disobeying the law.

51 In the Greek text this could be a statement as in *you are paying taxes*, or it can be a command to pay taxes.

52 There are two Greek words used for taxes in the Greek text that have no English equivalent. One word refers to a tax levied on assets owned. The

other refers to a tax levied on goods purchased as well as on the use of services. However, the two words together cover every kind of tax.

53 Literally, *one another.*

54 Literally, *stumble.* This is certainly a state of spiritual decline.

55 Literally, *Christ Jesus.*

56 Derived from Romans 5:1.

57 The Greek word, *Amen,* means *truly.*

58 Literally, *worthy of saints.*

59 Literally, *in the Lord.*

60 The earliest Greek manuscripts do not contain verse 24.

61 Literally, *the Lord Jesus Christ.*

62 The Greek text does not reflect a wish but exclaims a fact.

63 Literally, *our Lord Jesus Christ.*

64 The Greek word generally means *to make complete.* It was often used to describe the process of mending torn nets. Paul was notorious for metaphors and perhaps has this in mind as the Corinthian Christians were torn with division and needed mending.

65 The Greek word translated *know* refers to a personal knowledge as opposed to a general knowledge. There is a difference between knowing about God and knowing Him in a personal way. See Matthew 7:23 where this word is used by Jesus in this way, "I never knew you." See also John 17:3.

66 Derived from verse 31.

67 Some Greek manuscripts read *mystery* and others read *testimony.* Both have good support. It is my opinion that the reading *mystery* has slightly better attestation.

68 Most translations state that the rulers did not understand or know this mystery. The Greek word is the same one that is used in 1:21. It refers to knowing in a personal way.

69 Derived from 2:12.

70 Paul is not talking about each believer's body as being a dwelling place of the Spirit. He is referring to the local church body in Corinth.

71 Literally, *that which is written.* It is unclear whether Paul was referring to his own writing, the Scriptures that he quoted, or Scripture in general.

72 In verse 7 Paul's audience changes from the whole church to an individual, as is clarified in the Greek text, by using *you* in the singular and using verbs in the second person singular. He returns to addressing the whole church in the next verse.

73 Paul must be referring to the stepmother and not the natural mother because of the way it is phrased.

74 Literally, *the one who practiced this.*

75 Derived from the following context.

76 The Greek word is most often used to refer to sexual immorality, but in this case it refers to a general lifestyle of sin. Most versions of the Bible use the term *immoral* here.

77 The title, *the Way*, is derived from Acts 9:2. When Paul refers to outsiders, he means those who have no identification with the Christian faith. Thus all outsiders are unbelievers. However, when Paul refers to insiders, he means those who have identified with the Christian faith, which could include unbelievers. Just because one claims to be a believer does not mean that the person is one.

78 Literally, *the brother or the sister.*

79 Literally, *the Lord's.*

80 Scholars are divided as to whether Paul is speaking about a father's behavior toward his virgin daughter or a man's behavior toward the virgin he is courting. Verse 38 clarifies which one to whom Paul is referring.

81 Many translations read *marry* instead of *giving in marriage*. The Greek language has a word that means *to marry* and a related word that means *to give in marriage*. Both words can be seen in Matthew 22:30. Because Paul uses the Greek word that means *to give in marriage*, he must be talking about the father's behavior toward his virgin daughter.

82 Derived from verse 9.

83 The Greek text uses a word that means to know in a personal way, by experience. See 1:21 note.

84 The Greek word translated *love* emphasizes acting for the good of another without any regard for self.

85 In the Greek language, the answer to rhetorical questions are given in the text. The three questions here expect the answer of yes.

86 The rhetorical questions here expect the answer of no as the Greek text makes plain. See previous note.

87 The two questions in this verse are rhetorical, expecting the same answer of yes.

88 Literally, *the conscience of the other*. This cannot be the conscience of the unbeliever serving the meal, but the conscience of another believer. Perhaps there were others present at this meal that could not in good conscience eat meat that had been sacrificed to idols. In this case abstaining is best so as not to be a stumbling block.

89 It is possible to understand the term *angel* as a human messenger, which is how it is translated in Mark 1:2. It is possible to understand the term *angel* as referring to a bad angel or a demon, which is how it is understood in Revelation 12:7. Most likely it refers to the good angels who are present with us during Christian gatherings. These angels observe us (1 Corinthians 4:9), minister to us (Hebrews 1:14), and worship Jesus (Hebrews 1:6). Jesus has a special presence when believers gather in His name (Matthew 18:20). This presence we cannot

see, but angels can. Thus the angels around us can join believers in corporate worship. But if allowances are made for men or women to go against their created design and order, they are no longer gathered in Christ's name. His special presence is not there for the angels to enjoy.

90 Literally, *in the Lord.*

91 The preliminary action of looking within before taking the Lord's Supper is translated as *examine* by most translations. The Greek word Paul chose was used in the testing of metals and so means *to approve after testing.* The idea is that one must have deep introspection and make things right within.

92 Literally, *a number sleep.*

93 Literally, *with the world.*

94 Derived from verse 20.

95 Implied.

96 The reader should note that the present tense and not the past tense is used in reference to these gifts. Unlike the gifts in Romans 12:7,8, these gifts cannot be possessed all the time but only during the time of operation.

97 Derived from Acts 2:6-8. These are languages that the speaker has not learned and therefore cannot speak unless the Spirit gives them that gift.

98 This phrase is often translated *just as He wills.* The Greek word does not refer to a wish but to a determined plan. God's wishes may or may not happen, but His determined plans are always fulfilled. A person cannot just decide to speak in tongues, or prophesy, or heal. The Spirit decides this.

99 In the Greek text, all the questions expect a negative answer.

100 The topic of chapter 13 is love. The Greek word is *agape* which refers to a love that acts for the good of another without any thought for self. Thus I have translated it here and throughout the chapter as *selfless love* or *unselfish love.*

101 In this chapter the apostle Paul makes a distinction between speaking in tongues as a genuine gift of the Spirit and speaking in tongues as nonsensical babbling. The gift of tongues was a gift in which words were spoken to those who could understand those words (Acts 2:4-11). But nonsensical babbling were words spoken to God. He does not condemn these emotional utterances, only their display. He equates the genuine gift of tongues with prophecy and so urges them to be zealous for prophecy. The purpose of the gift of tongues was to speak a message to an unbeliever (verse 22). Babbling was just self-edifying and Paul instructed them to keep this between themselves and God (verse 28).

102 Literally, *the church.*

103 Literally, *you will be speaking into the air.*

104 Literally, *I will be a barbarian.* A barbarian was one who could only speak his own tribal language, unable to speak the trade language of Greek. This term developed from the frail attempts to imitate the sound these foreigners made when trying to communicate, *bar-bar.* The Greek word is *barbaros.* This term very quickly came to be used in a derogatory sense, but not so by the New Testament writers.

105 Who is this hypothetical person Paul singles out in the church service? Translations vary: *the ungifted, the unlearned, an inquirer.* The word refers to one who is a private person, not part of a community. In this context this person would be an unbeliever outside the church community who comes to a church meeting to find out about the Christian faith.

106 Implied.

107 The action of talking is in the Greek present tense which emphasizes ongoing action. Obviously Paul is not forbidding all women to talk, for he already instructed how women were to pray and prophesy in a church service in chapter 11. The command to keep silent is situational of wives. If this were a problem among men, he would have told them to keep quiet as well. Evidently wives were chatting while someone else had the floor. Even if they really wanted to learn something, they were not to ask their husbands during the church service but at home.

108 Implied.

109 Paul uses an abundance of pronouns to refer to God the Father and Jesus. I took the liberty to identify the pronoun used in this phrase as referring to the person whom is called God the Father.

110 Literally, *by your boasting which I have in Christ Jesus our Lord.* This is an oath to emphasize the truth of facing death on a daily basis. It is similar to today's practice of swearing on one's mother's grave.

111 Implied.

112 This is not stating that the resurrection body lacks a physical form. In 2:14,15 the same words are used to contrast the believer with the unbeliever. The unbeliever is call the natural person, and the believer is called the spiritual person. These words do not describe form but condition. The unbeliever is natural because of the sinful condition. The believer is spiritual because of salvation. Likewise, the physical body with which we are born dies because its condition is mortal, but the resurrection body has a spiritual condition which is exempt from the effects of sin.

113 Derived from verses 52 and 53.

114 Verse 53 is actually repeated word for word here, but I have summed it up in two words, *the aforementioned.*

115 Paul assumes the reader knows that the collection is for the saints in Jerusalem. I have added the word *Jerusalem* in this verse for the benefit of the modern reader.

116 The Greek word translated as *love* is *phileo*, which refers to having affection for someone as a friend.

117 The meaning of the word *anathema* literally means to *place up* and originally referred to an offering to a deity hung on a wall either as a blessing or as a curse. Eventually the negative meaning dominated. Thus one who was anathematized was considered to be cut off from God.

118 The meaning of *Maranatha* is *our Lord come.*

119 The Greek text does not reflect a wish but an exclamation of fact. The Lord's grace and Paul's love was with the Corinthian Christians. See 1:3.

120 The Greek text does not reflect a wish but exclaims a fact.

121 This is a rhetorical question that expects the answer of no as is plain in the Greek text.

122 The action of writing a letter was often put in the past tense since it was complete by the time the reader read the letter. Therefore, many translators will translate as *I am writing* instead of *I wrote*. Scholars are divided over whether the writing referred to in this verse is the present letter or a previous one. I think Paul is referring to his previous letter where he dealt with sinful issues. He was giving them time to straighten out so that when he came again there would be no need for correction.

123 Titus as the messenger of Paul's previous letter is added here. That information is derived from 7:5-8. This passage would not make sense without this knowledge.

124 Titus met Paul in Macedonia (7:5,6). This is his response to that meeting.

125 More literally, *among those who are perishing.*

126 The Greek text is in the form of a rhetorical question, *how will the ministry of the Spirit not be more glorious?*

127 The Greek word Paul uses for knowledge refers to a personal knowledge gained by experience. Here he is referring to the salvation experience where God causes His glory to shine out of what was originally a dark heart.

128 Literally, *but not abandoned.*

129 Paul does not specifically state that the quote comes from the Psalms. See Psalm 116:10.

130 Paul uses the term *Belial*, a title traditional Jews gave Satan.

131 The words *to sin* are not in the Greek text. Paul is not referring to physical death and life, but the shared experience of dying to sin and living to God as he points out in 5:15. He urges the Corinthians to make room for him and Timothy as they made room for them in their hearts, not yoking themselves with unbelievers but with them (6:11-18).

132 Derived from the next verse.

133 Literally, *Just as it is written.*

134 Literally, *apostles*. The basic meaning of apostle is *one who is sent out.* That is the meaning here. These brothers were not apostles in the same sense as Paul.

135 Derived from 8:11.
136 The term *blessing* translates a Greek word where we get our word eulogy. It literally means *a good word* and generally refers to a verbal blessing. Here it refers to a financial blessing.
137 Derived from 8:10.
138 Paul most certainly has Proverbs 11:24 in mind.
139 The Greek word that Paul uses here is the same metaphor used in 1 Corinthians 9:7 of one who serves as a soldier. Although Paul does not specifically say that the service is to God, it is obvious that is what he means. So, I have taken the liberty to make this plain.
140 Derived from 10:13.
141 Literally, *did not accept.*
142 Derived from 11:7.
143 See Acts 14:19,20.
144 Scholars are divided over whether this phrase goes with what precedes or what follows.
145 Scholars seem to be puzzled as to what the thorn in the flesh was, but Paul tells us – *a messenger of Satan.* The word *Satan* means, *one who opposes.* Everywhere Paul carried the gospel he was opposed. Certainly Satan was behind it, but God had already declared to Paul that he would suffer greatly for His name (Acts 9:16). Paul has described this opposition already (11:23-27) and sums it up in one word, weaknesses (11:30). He makes it clear that the thorn in the flesh are weaknesses (12:9) and even lists them again (12:10).
146 The word Paul chooses literally means, *to set a tent upon*, with the idea of living in it. Here Paul pictures the power of God living in him in a visible way as he serves Him in all the adversities listed in verse 10.
147 The Greek text has a preposition preceding each word except for the last one, *in persecutions and distresses,* which could be giving a further description of the persecutions – distressful persecutions.
148 This question expects the answer no.
149 This is really a question, expecting the answer no.
150 The Greek text is a question, expecting the answer yes.
151 The Greek word used by Paul has multiple meanings. It most commonly means to rejoice. However, it can also be used as a greeting (Matthew 28:9) or as a farewell, as here, although scholars are divided over its meaning here.
152 Literally, *a holy kiss.* The word *holy* means *set apart.* Paul was commanding the readers to greet one another in a way that was different than the customary greeting which was often done without thought. Christians ought to greet one another in a meaningful way.
153 The Greek text lacks a verb, which is a way of exclaiming a fact. If it were a wish, a verb in the optative mode would have been used as in 1 Thessalonians 5:23.

154 Implied. Although Jesus is a man, Paul stresses the deity of Jesus by saying that his apostleship did not come from a human source.

155 The Greek text does not reflect a wish which is usually expressed with a verb in the optative mode. Here, there is no verb in the Greek text and so should be understood as an exclamation of fact.

156 Literally, *Jesus Christ.*

157 Literally, *in Judaism.*

158 Literally, *to the apostles before me.* Paul is referring to the original apostles chosen by Christ during His earthly ministry.

159 It could be misunderstood that Paul went to Jerusalem three years after returning to Damascus. In order to avoid this misunderstanding, I have used poetic license to mark the three year period from the time that God revealed Jesus to him.

160 The word *apostle* usually refers to those directly chosen by Christ. A few times it is used to refer to anyone sent out, such as Barnabas (Acts 14:14) and certain brothers that accompanied Paul in his travels (2 Corinthians 8:23 where it is translated as *messengers*). Most believe this James to be the elder of the Jerusalem church and so an apostle in the wider sense. Few believe this to be an apostle in a strict sense. If the latter is true, he would be James the son of Alpheus, a cousin to Jesus.

161 Literally, *churches in Christ.* We might think it strange for Paul to describe churches as being in Christ. But the word *church* was used to refer to Jewish gatherings as well.

162 The preposition can be understood in two ways: after fourteen years or during a fourteen year period. The Galatian letter was written prior to the Council of Jerusalem recorded in Acts 15 (49 or 50 AD). We know this because there is no mention of the letter from that council which went out to all the Gentile churches to deal with the Gentiles' relationship to the Mosaic Law. If the fourteen year interval was after the three years in Arabia, that would put Paul's conversion too close to the crucifixion of Christ. Therefore, I chose to translate it as *during a fourteen year span.*

163 Literally, *not even for an hour,* a Greek idiom meaning not for any time at all.

164 Literally, *the circumcised.*

165 Literally, *the truth of the gospel.* No doubt the truth to which Paul is referring is grace.

166 Scholars are divided over what verses comprise what Paul told to Peter's face in everyone's presence. Was it just verses 15,16 or was it the rest of chapter 2? I have opted for the latter, placing end quotes at the end of the chapter.

167 Paul is not referring to the Mosaic Law specifically but to law in general. See Romans 2:12 note. He gives a general principle here, then applies it specifically to the Mosaic Law in chapter 3.

168 The word *justified* means *to be declared righteous.*

169 Literally, *May it not happen.*
170 The argument is hard to follow. Paul is speaking about a person who has come to understand that righteousness comes by faith in Christ and not by keeping rules. If this person rebuilds a system of works as a means of righteousness after tearing it down as that means, then he only proves himself to be a sinner.
171 Scholars are divided as to whether this is a statement or a command. If it is a command, Paul is telling them to learn this truth. If it is a statement, Paul is appealing to their own personal experience when receiving Christ. The Greek word translated as *know* means *to know personally.* See John 17:3 notes.
172 Poetic elaboration. This is a quote from Habakkuk 2:4. See Romans 1:17 notes.
173 Poetic elaboration. Paul is quoting Leviticus 18:5.
174 Literally, *Jesus Christ.*
175 Many versions translate as *the Law*, referring to the Law of Moses. However, there is no *the* in the Greek text (see Romans 2:12 notes). Jesus was under law in general, which included the Mosaic Law.
176 The Greek word is often translated *born* in most versions of the Bible, but technically it means *to be* or *exist.* His earthly existence began in the womb, not when He was born.
177 Poetic elaboration on the word translated as *know.* See John 17:3 notes.
178 Literally, *they.* Paul is referring to those people who were trying to draw away the Galatian Christians by a different gospel (see 1:6 and 3:1).
179 Poetic elaboration summarizing Paul's analogy that he makes in the next several verses.
180 The last two lines of this stanza are poetic elaboration on the meaning of the word hope. When it comes to the things of God, hope is a certainty. See Romans 5:5.
181 The language employed by the Greek text is a wish that falls short of reality. See Romans 9:3 notes for the same construction.
182 The word *enmity* is in the plural in the Greek text, which I have reflected with the words *without measure.*
183 The word *unrighteous* is not in the Greek text. But there is a righteous jealousy. See 2 Corinthians 11:2.
184 This word was originally used to refer to a celebration of the wine god. The word eventually became used to refer to any feast that honored a pagan god.
185 Implied. See Romans 6:6.
186 Literally, *the law of Christ.* No doubt Paul is referring to the commandment of love Jesus gave in John 13:34.
187 Most translations read similar to either *lose heart* or *grow weary.* The Greek word is literally *in badness.* The contrast is to doing good. So the idea is not to give in to doing bad.

188 The phrase *to the utmost* is poetic elaboration in an attempt to distinguish these Jews from the Judaizers who insisted that the whole Law of Moses be kept in addition to professing to follow Christ. These circumcised ones were Jewish people who did not continue the sacrifices or hold to the priestly system because they understood that Christ was their sacrifice and their High Priest. They just did not want to be persecuted by the Judaizers and so pushed circumcision upon Gentiles.

189 This is not a wish but an exclamation of fact as the Greek text makes clear. See Galatians 1:3 and 2 Corinthians 13:14 notes.

190 Somewhat of a repeat of a portion of Galatians 1:3.

191 The meaning of *Amen* is truly.

192 There are many early manuscripts that omit the words *in Ephesus*. One church father states that this letter was to the saints in Laodicea. Other church fathers vary in their quotes of this verse as including or excluding *in Ephesus*. It is possible that this letter was intended to be a general letter to all churches. As it was copied and sent to a specific church, the city name was specified.

193 This is not a wish but an exclamation of fact as the Greek text makes clear. See Galatians 1:3 and 2 Corinthians 13:14 notes.

194 Translations use the term *heavenly places*. This is slightly different in form than the common Greek word for heaven. The word is used to refer to the places where demons are (Ephesians 6:12). We know that demons are no longer in heaven (see Revelation 12:7-9). This word was used in secular Greek to refer to the various dwelling places of the gods. These places were not visible to humans. Therefore, the word is better defined as the unseen places of the spiritual world. The context would have to determine if a specific unseen place is meant. Although plural, the word can have a singular meaning just like the word *heavens* does in the Greek.

195 Paul is implying that the gospel was designed to first come to the Jews and then to the Gentiles.

196 Literally, *the Lord Jesus*.

197 This is the same word used in 1:3 translated there as *unseen places*. Since in this context we know the unseen place to be heaven, I have translated it that way here.

198 In this verse, although the phrase *is His seat* is absent in the Greek text, it is certainly understood from verses 20,21 that Christ is seated at the Father's right hand with authority.

199 See 1:3 notes.

200 This refers to spiritual authorities. See 1:3 notes.

201 Paul is referring to the specific time God called them to salvation in Christ.

202 Scholars are divided over whether Paul is referring to Christ's descent to the earth by becoming human or to His descent into Hades between

the time of His death and resurrection (see 1 Peter 3:18,19). The Greek text can be understood as *the lower place called the earth* or *the place lower than the earth.*

203 The verse can either be translated *to fill all things* or *to fulfill all things.* An argument for the former is Ephesians 1:23. An argument for the latter is the language Jesus commonly used of fulfilling the Scriptures.

204 The Greek word translated as *sealed* refers to a stamp of ownership.

205 This is translated by most versions as *thanksgiving* or something similar. The Greek word is the combination of a prefix meaning *good* and the word *grace.* Thanksgiving naturally developed out of this meaning as the word *grace* means *gift* and thanks was a good gift to give. But perhaps Paul is referring to the most basic meaning of the word here, *pleasant speech,* which is found in secular Greek literature.

206 Paul uses the adversative *but* to show that the point is not with Jesus as Savior of the body but with Jesus as head of the body.

207 *They tend* is derived from the next verse.

208 Literally, *since we are parts of His body.*

209 Poetic elaboration on the meaning of the word *mystery.*

210 Most translations read, *fathers.* However, the word also means *parents* which every translation renders in Hebrews 11:23. Paul has addressed husbands and wives. He later addresses slaves and masters. It is reasonable to conclude that here he is addressing children and parents. The New Jerusalem Bible translates it this way. A strong argument against this translation is that if Paul meant parents he would have used the same Greek word he used in the command *children, obey your parents.*

211 See 1:3 notes.

212 Most translations read, *all the saints.* The word *saint* literally means *one set apart.*

213 The grammatical structure Paul uses supplies no verb, which was a Greek way of making an exclamation. See 1:2 notes.

214 This is not a wish, but an exclamation of fact. See 1:2 notes.

215 Literally, *Christ Jesus's.*

216 Literally, *saints in Christ Jesus.*

217 This is not a wish but an exclamation of fact as the Greek text makes clear. See 2 Corinthians 13:14 and Galatians 1:3 notes.

218 Literally, *Christ Jesus.*

219 Scholars are divided over whether Paul is referring to people or places in this verse.

220 Many translations translate this as *even if I am...* which may communicate a mere possibility. However, this is a kind of conditional sentence that assumes it to be fact. A drink offering was added to a sacrifice as something pleasing to God (see Numbers 15:5). The sacrifice was the Philippian Christians' service and the drink offering was

Paul's imprisonment for the cause of Christ. Although an unpleasant experience, it was reason to rejoice.

221 Poetic elaboration on the word *know* at the beginning of the verse. This word translates a word that means *to know personally.* Acts 16 records Timothy as accompanying Paul to Philippi when this church was planted. Timothy was also sent there as Acts 19:22 states. See also Acts 20:1-6. They observed Timothy firsthand.

222 *Whom you sent* is poetic elaboration on the word apostle which literally means *one sent out.*

223 The word *law* lacks the Greek article *the.* So, Paul is referring to the body of law that the Pharisees kept, the Mosaic Law and the additional traditional laws. Therefore, I have taken license to call it *Jewish law.*

224 The Greek word Paul chose can mean *to follow* or *to live in an orderly manner.* Paul's point is that believers, regardless of where they are on the spiritual maturity scale, must never go backwards but always progress spiritually.

225 The words *not far away* are poetic elaboration on the meaning of the word *near.* When speaking of events, the word *near* is used to mean near as far as time is concerned (e.g. Matthew 24:32). When used of persons, places, or things it means near as far as space (e.g. John 3:23). The Greek text literally reads: *the Lord is near.* How near is He? He is present within us. See Romans 10:8 for *near* being defined as *within.*

226 The most basic translation is *the peace of God.* This can be understood as a subjective or objective peace. I understand this not to be a feeling (subjective peace) but a fact of our relationship (objective peace). We have peace with God because of what Jesus did on the cross. We are no longer at odds with God (see Romans 5:1). Worries cause our minds to focus on troubling possibilities. The peace we have with God guards our minds and hearts from worry by focusing us on the certainties of our relationship to Him.

227 Paul is using terms of bookkeeping. He started this picture back in verse 15 concerning, literally, *the account of giving and receiving.*

228 This is not a wish but an exclamation of fact as the Greek text makes clear. See 2 Corinthians 13:14 and Galatians 1:3 notes.

229 Poetic elaboration on the grammatical structure in the Greek text. Paul is giving an exclamation of fact. See 2 Corinthians 13:14 and Galatians 1:3 notes.

230 Literally, *grace to you and peace from God our Father.* The grammatical structure of the Greek text reveals this as an exclamation of fact. See 2 Corinthians 13:14 and Galatians 1:3 notes.

231 Poetic elaboration on the meaning of the word *love,* which is *agape* in the Greek text.

232 The Greek word translated as *knowing* has to do with a personal knowledge as opposed to an intellectual knowledge. See John 17:3

notes. This same word is used in the previous verse in a context that plainly shows that this knowledge has to do with personal experience as opposed to just a collection of facts.

233 The word *redemption* was used to refer to a payment that was made to release a slave as well as a payment made on a debtor's behalf.

234 This line is poetic elaboration on the meaning of firstborn. Firstborn has only two meanings. See Romans 8:29 notes.

235 This passage begins with a word translated by versions as "for" or "because." An explanation or reason is being given for Jesus's authority over creation. This last line sums up that one word and its correlation with the previous verse.

236 The word *firstborn* is in apposition to the word *beginning*. In other words, it is defining in what sense Jesus is the beginning. In many contexts of the Greek text this word, translated here as *beginning,* refers to rulers (e.g. Luke 12:11; Romans 8:38; 1 Corinthians 15:24; Colossians 1:16). So Jesus is the beginning in the sense of being firstborn, that is, supreme (see Romans 8:29 notes).

237 Many miss the point of this phrase that many translations render as *firstborn from the dead.* Jesus was counted among the dead when He was crucified and buried. His authority as firstborn was given Him when He rose from the dead (see Psalm 89:27; Matthew 28:18).

238 The emphasis in the Greek text is on the phrase *through Him,* referring to Christ. This verse is used by some to say that eventually everyone will be saved. However, the point is that only through Christ is there reconciliation. This truth applies not to some things, but applies to all things.

239 The literal meaning of the word *church* is *called out ones.* The implication is that believers in Christ have been called out from the world.

240 The Greek word emphasizes a knowledge gained by personal experience.

241 *As I've said* is poetic elaboration. This is a repetition of the idea in 1:19.

242 The word *sliced* is literally *circumcised.* The word *circumcise* means *to cut around.* Here the picture is of the sinful nature being removed. This idea is repeated in verse 13.

243 The metaphor in the Greek text is that of stripping off clothes.

244 Derived from 2:23.

245 Some Greek manuscripts read *the things he has not seen,* the earliest being a 5th century copy. All the copies earlier than that, which number only three for this scripture, read *the things that are seen.*

246 Literally, *God the Father.*

247 This word is translated as *fathers* by most translations but can mean *parents* as it does in Hebrews 11:23. See Ephesians 6:4 note.

248 The information of returning Onesimus is taken from the letter to Philemon. Onesimus was a runaway slave who had somehow made his way to Paul and had come to Christ.

249 Paul was imprisoned in Rome during the time he wrote this letter.

250 This is an exclamation of fact, not a mere wish, as the Greek text makes clear. See 2 Corinthians 13:14 and Galatians 1:3 notes.

251 This is not a wish but an exclamation of fact as the Greek text makes clear. See 2 Corinthians 13:14 and Galatians 1:3 notes.

252 The Greek text is more literally, *just as you know what kind we were to you because of you.* Paul is making a comparison that just as he, Silas, and Timothy knew of their election due to the fruit they exhibited, so the Thessalonian Christians know that God chose Paul, Silas, and Timothy by the fruit they exhibited while spreading the gospel there.

253 Translations vary because the Greek copies of this verse have two different words, *infant* (Greek – nēpioi) or *gentle* (Greek – ēpioi). Note that the two Greek words vary by one letter (n). It is plausible that the first letter (n) of the word for infant was accidentally dropped which produced the variant reading. It is equally plausible that (n) was accidentally added to the word for gentle, since the Greek word preceding it ends in an (n). If the original was *gentle,* then the metaphor makes perfect sense. If the original was *infant,* then Paul is giving two metaphors, the first of an infant, the second of a nursing mother.

254 Literally, *in Christ Jesus.*

255 Translations vary between *to the end, to the uttermost,* and *at last.* The problem of language is that Paul put the arrival of wrath as a past event when it is yet future. However, Paul also put our future glorification as a past event in Romans 8:29. It was not uncommon to put future certainties in terms of the past to stress its certainty. Paul is referring to the final wrath of God upon sin.

256 This is a first class conditional sentence in the Greek language which assumes the condition to be true, whether true or not. In this context it is true due to the report of Timothy.

257 Literally, *our God and Father.*

258 Literally, *our Lord Jesus.*

259 Three examples of sanctified living are given: (1) abstaining from fornication, (2) obtaining property properly, and (3) honest business practices.

260 Some scholars think Paul is referring a person's wife. But Paul is not instructing just husbands, but *each of you.* Others think that Paul is referring to a person's body. But the action verb in the Greek has to do with obtaining or acquiring. The Greek word in question is commonly used to refer to a vessel or instrument of any material. Revelation 18:11-14 uses the same Greek word to refer to merchandise. The sense is that Christians are not to obtain anything just because they have a deep desire for it. The parameters for obtaining something as our own is holiness and honor.

261 Literally, *we who are still alive.*

262 The words *of hope* are not in this verse but are derived from verse 13.

263 This line is poetic elaboration. Obviously Paul does not mean to refer to the times and the seasons of anything but specifically those events that he just explained in chapter 4 pertaining to the resurrection of the dead and the coming of Christ.

264 Derived from verse 4. The day of the Lord only overtakes unbelievers like a thief. Believers will welcome this day.

265 Literally, *as the rest.*

266 More literally, *when it is night.*

267 The tense in the Greek refers to a one time action as opposed to a continual action. This is not to say that we cannot put this armor on more than once. The point is not to put it on, take it off, put it on, take it off, etc. The point is to put it on and keep it on.

268 Literally, *Christ Jesus.*

269 Poetic elaboration on the meaning of the word *holy.* Paul was urging them to go beyond the customary greeting of the culture. See 2 Corinthians 13:12 notes.

270 Literally, *all the brothers.*

271 The Greek text lacks the verb and so is not a wish but an exclamation of fact. See 2 Corinthians 13:14 and Galatians 1:3 notes.

272 The word order in the Greek text is *Paul, Silas, and Timothy.*

273 This is not a wish but an exclamation of fact as the Greek text makes clear. See 2 Corinthians 13:14 and Galatians 1:3 notes.

274 The word *apostasy* is a Greek word adopted into the English language. The Greek word is a combination of a prefix meaning *from* and a word meaning *to stand,* thus giving the idea of abandoning. English dictionaries define apostasy as a rejection of one's religious beliefs in order to follow another belief. The Greek word, *apostasia,* is only used one other time in the New Testament. In Acts 21:21 it refers to the act of Jews abandoning the teachings of Moses that they once held and embracing contradictory teachings. Therefore, the apostasy in Christianity refers to a mass abandonment of Christianity (by those who embraced Christianity) in order to follow another system. This may correspond to Revelation 13:14-18 when the world will be divided into two distinct religious camps, those who follow the beast and those who follow Christ. There will be no nominal Christians or hypocrites in that time.

275 Verse 6 uses a neuter participle, which I have rendered as *the restraining power.* Verse 7 uses the same participle but in the masculine gender, referring to the person doing the restraining. Scholars debate the meaning of the restraining power and the person restraining. Paul did not give any explanation of what he meant because, as he states in verse 6, the Thessalonians already knew about the restraining power. Verse 7 goes on to say that He restrains *until He gets Himself out of the way.*

The verb used in the Greek text is a word that simply means *to become*. Some translations render this verb in a passive sense, as the Restrainer being taken out of the way by someone else. But the verb is not in the passive voice but the middle voice which means that the Restrainer is acting with reference to Himself. Thus, His action makes it so that He becomes out of the way.

276 The word is translated as *killed* by many translations, but it more literally means *to take away*. The context determines what is being taken away. Revelation 19:20,21 states that at Christ's coming this person, better known as the false prophet, will not be killed by His coming, only his army will be. It states that He will be thrown alive into the Lake of Fire. Therefore, he is not killed by the Lord's breath, but he is taken away.

277 Some early Greek copies have the reading, *from the beginning*. The Greek word for first fruits differs only by one letter. Scholars are equally divided over which reading is the original. If *first fruits* is original, Paul is referring to the first harvest for salvation. The second harvest is for condemnation. These two harvests are pictured in Revelation 14:15-20.

278 Literally, *the sanctification of the spirit*. A Greek reader could understand this phrase in two ways: (1) the sanctification done by the Holy Spirit, or (2) the sanctification done to the human spirit. Both ideas are biblical.

279 Literally, the word *King* is literally Christ.

280 Literally, *our Lord Jesus Christ*.

281 The Greek text literally is, *the love of God* and *the patience of Christ*. A Greek reader could understand that God and Christ are to be the object of love and patience, or that the Christian is to exhibit the same love and patience that God and Christ did.

282 The Lord's presence is not a wish here but an exclamation of fact as the Greek text makes clear. See 2 Corinthians 13:14 and Galatians 1:3 notes.

283 Literally, *our Lord Jesus Christ's grace*.

284 This is not a wish but an exclamation of fact as the Greek text makes clear. See 2 Corinthians 13:14 and Galatians 1:3 notes.

285 The word *heavenly* is poetic elaboration.

286 Literally, *the goal of the instruction*. Paul uses the same root word as he did in verse 3 for Timothy's act of instructing others. So, the instruction to which Paul is referring here is Timothy's act of instructing others. Therefore, I have translated it as *the goal of your instruction*.

287 Literally, *Christ Jesus*.

288 This phrase is very vague in the Greek text. It literally reads, *in its own times*. Because the word *times* is in the plural, it cannot be referring to one season or event but several. The word *times* refers to opportunities (see Ephesians 5:16 and Colossians 4:5 for this same Greek word carrying the idea of opportunity). The message, that Jesus is the ransom for all, is the testimony to be given as opportunities present themselves.

This exact Greek phrase is used in 1 Timothy 6:15 (see notes there) and Titus 1:3.

289 The dress code of worldly women who advertised themselves as sexual objects was the attire described in this verse. One must look beyond the rule and at the principle that Paul is giving. Christian women must dress in a way that reflects godliness not worldliness.

290 The word *quietness* does not necessarily mean absolute silence. This word has to do with order as the next phrase makes clear, *submissive in every way*. See 2 Thessalonians 3:12 where the same Greek word is used to describe the manner a person is to work.

291 This interesting commentary on the fall depicts Adam as fully aware of the serpent's trickery. He was not deceived, where Eve was fooled. Eve took the role as teacher and leader over Adam, and Adam let her! The Greek text indicates that Eve's state of being in sin was an ongoing state. Paul does not comment on Adam's wrong because the subject matter deals with why a woman is not to take the role of teacher or leader over a man.

292 This passage has many interpretations. The subject of who will be saved is unexpressed but requires a singular subject in the Greek text. Yet, the next sentence requires a plural subject. Literally it reads, [she] *will be saved if* [they] *remain*. I understand that Paul is applying what happened to Eve to the female race in general. Therefore, *she* would refer to women as a singular entity – woman or the female race. And *they* would naturally follow. We do this often in English when referring to a group. *The group listened to the joke, but they refused to laugh*. And so the female race will be saved if they remain in faith. The context determines what they will be saved from - deception.

293 This description is translated by many versions as the husband of one wife. The Greek text literally reads, *a man of one woman*. This is not a requirement of the marital status of an overseer, but a description of his philosophy and practice. Whether married or not, he must practice and teach that a man must belong to only one woman at a time. This means he must stand against promiscuity, adultery, homosexuality, polygamy, bigamy, and the like and stand for the sanctity of marriage between one man and one woman. He must do this in word and deed. Therefore, he must be a one-woman kind of man.

294 The Greek text does not contain the words, *the church*, but reads *those outside* or simply *outsiders*.

295 More literally, *shame* [and] *snare of the Devil*. The word *and* is not giving an additional idea but is closely associating the two. The snare of the Devil is to cause leaders to fall into shame.

296 The qualifications of this group of women is found in the middle of the qualifications for deacons. It is hard to imagine that only the wives of deacons would have to qualify and not wives of overseers. Therefore,

many apply this section to the wives of both deacons and overseers. However, the Greek word for wife and for woman is the same. It is often distinguished by either putting a possessive before it (e.g. your wife), or by putting the article *the* before it. Here there is neither. Because this is in the middle of the qualifications for deacons, it would be natural to understand this to refer to women deacons. The Greek word for deacon was applied to Phoebe in Romans 16:1.

297 The Greek word is the verb form of confession, which literally means *to speak the same, to agree.* In this sentence it is an adverb and so the mystery is confessedly great. It seems that what follows was some kind of confession that was recited from memory by congregations.

298 The Greek word is often translated as *angel* but simply means messenger (see Revelation 2:1 notes). Due to the progression of this hymn, it seems better to understand this word as referring to the people who saw the appearances of the resurrected Jesus and went on to be preachers of the gospel story.

299 The term *later times* does not refer to the last days which began when Jesus sent the Holy Spirit and extends until the coming of Christ (see Acts 2:17). The word used is *later.* It is a word of comparison. It is later than something else. That "something else" must refer to the time that the Spirit prophesied this. The Spirit evidently said this early on in Paul's ministry. Paul now sees it as fulfilled as he nears the end of his ministry.

300 Paul is referring to the godliness mentioned in verse 8.

301 Poetic elaboration derived from verse 1 of this chapter. The word *save* means to rescue and the context determines what it is from. This is not referring to Timothy saving himself and his hearers from sin's penalty. Timothy was already saved in this sense. However, deception is a constant threat to all believers. That is the context of this entire chapter. Teaching and practicing the teachings of God will save Timothy and his hearers from deception.

302 The Greek text literally reads *a woman of one man.* This could mean that the widow could not have been married more than once. However, a similar description is given for overseers in 1 Timothy 3:2, and no one would disqualify an overseer for remarrying if he became a widower. Grammatically, *one man* can simply be a description of *woman.* This refers to the philosophy and practice of the widow. She is a one-man kind of woman. She must teach and demonstrate by her own life the sanctity of marriage between one man and one woman. See notes for 1 Timothy 3:2.

303 Paul addresses the issue of the church supporting younger widows who were most likely without children. Paul implies that some were pledging that they would remain celibate for Christ's sake if supported by the church and would dedicate themselves to serving Christ. However,

he directs Timothy to not put them on the register for church support since they most likely will violate their pledge of celibacy and eventually get married. He also lists a host of other problems that was already occurring among them. He then directs younger widows not to pledge celibacy but to get married and raise a family.

304 Literally, *Satan.*

305 Some Greek copies record both male and female believers as being addressed.

306 This line is poetic elaboration concerning the laying on of hands. This has to do with approving individuals as elders, deacons, and possibly even the supported widows. All must be qualified. The next command is not disconnected with the first. *Neither contribute to others' sins.* Approving people without qualifying them could potentially lead to their downfall and the downfall of others because of their position of influence.

307 Poetic elaboration on the word *alone*. God alone is all that which is listed in verse 16.

308 The pseudo knowledge or false knowledge to which Paul is referring came from a group eventually called the Gnostics. The word *gnostic* means knowledge. This group claimed to be Christian but denied the basic tenets of the Christian faith.

309 The Greek word used here basically means *one who promises.* A secondary meaning developed to refer to a person who made a business out of proclaiming promises. Paul uses the secondary meaning here in a bad sense. Some made a business out of proclaiming the false knowledge of the Gnostics.

310 This is not a wish but an exclamation of fact as the Greek text makes clear. See 2 Corinthians 13:14 and Galatians 1:3 notes. Although Paul is writing just to Timothy, he abruptly ends this letter after showing that pseudo Christianity has nothing to offer. It is an exclamation to all true believers. All believers have God's grace with them.

311 This is not a wish but an exclamation of fact as the Greek text makes clear. See 2 Corinthians 13:14 and Galatians 1:3 notes.

312 Paul does not use a direct command as most versions translate (*do not be ashamed*), but a softened command (*let not yourself be ashamed*). I used poetic elaboration, translating *be ashamed* to *having a spirit of shame.*

313 It is easy to misunderstand how the phrase, *before the times of the ages,* is to be interpreted in this context. Some may picture God specifically giving Timothy and Paul grace before creation. However, what Paul means by *us* is not specific (as in Paul and Timothy) but generic (us, as in all believers). Also, the key phrase is *in Christ.* God decided that His gift of grace to all believers would be *in Christ* and not in works. No person could receive this grace except in Christ.

314 Literally, *Jesus Christ.*

315 Literally, *the Lord.*

316 Literally, *Christ Jesus.*

317 Literally, *through many witnesses.* It is difficult to make sense out of the literal translation since Paul directly taught Timothy. Translations will vary: *among many witnesses; in the presence of many witnesses; supported by many witnesses.* The idea is that Paul's teachings to Timothy were not unique but were verified by many witnesses.

318 Most translations give the understanding that the diligent farmer should be the first to receive from the crops he harvests. This understanding does not fit the previous illustrations. The first two illustrations focus on what the person ought to do, not what they ought to receive. Paul is making the same point with three different illustrations. The Greek text concerning the farmer can be understood another way. The word translated here as *first* by most translations in the sense of order (first, second, third) can mean *first* in the sense of rank (primary, foremost). A farmer must make hard work of primary importance in order to share in the crops. Laziness disqualifies him from sharing in the crops, just as not competing according to the rules disqualifies an athlete from the victory crown, and just as getting entangled in the things of life disqualifies a soldier from pleasing his commanding officer.

319 Literally, *what I am saying.*

320 Literally *will deny Him.*

321 Literally, *to deny Himself.*

322 *Through faith* is poetic elaboration. Obviously these men were not teaching that people missed the bodily resurrection. They were teaching that there is only a spiritual resurrection which occurs at the moment of faith in Christ and that there was no such thing as a future bodily resurrection.

323 The Greek word used here means *to know in a personal way.* The Lord does not know everyone this way (see Matthew 7:23). He only knows believers this way (see John 17:3).

324 Literally, *from these things.* This refers to the appeal in verse 19 to believers to depart from all that is wrong.

325 Scholars are divided over whether the last two lines refer to the Devil or to God or a mixture of the two. The Greek text literally reads, *being captured alive by him for that one's will.* If the last two lines refer to the Devil, it would be more natural to write, *being captured alive by him for his will.* The use of *that one* seems to more naturally apply to God or Christ. This is the vocabulary of Paul in this chapter (2 Timothy 2:12,13). On the other hand, the imagery of being captured alive is similar to the imagery of the Devil's snare. Therefore, some have interpreted the Devil as the one capturing alive and then connect doing God's will to escaping the snare. So the sense would be this: *they might escape the Devil's snare*

to do God's will after being captured alive by the Devil. The final option connects the idea of God granting repentance and God bringing them to the realization that they are in a trap, capturing them alive to do His will. All options are biblically sound. Which one Paul meant is difficult to know with full confidence. I have opted for the latter.

326 Jannes and Jambres, although not named in Exodus, are the traditional names given to the Egyptian magicians that tried to duplicate the miracles and plagues that Moses did.

327 Paul does not call Jannes and Jambres magicians, but simply designates them as *those ones.*

328 Literally, *the sacred writings.*

329 Derived from Romans 16:24.

330 The Greek text contains no verb in the ending of the letter. Therefore this is not a mere wish but an exclamation of fact. See 2 Corinthians 13:14 and Galatian 1:3 notes. Some English translations may lead the reader to think that this ending is to Timothy only. However, the first fact of the Lord's presence is to Timothy only since the word *your* is singular (*with your spirit*). The second fact of grace's presence is for all believers in Ephesus since the word *you* is in the plural (*with you all*).

331 Literally, *Jesus Christ's.*

332 The Greek word translated *knowledge* has a prefix that indicates fullness. The root word refers to a personal knowledge as opposed to merely knowing facts. See John 17:3 notes.

333 Paul is not requiring overseers to be married but to hold to the sanctity of marriage. See 1 Timothy 3:2 notes.

334 The word *faithful* is an adjective. Some translations may lead the reader to think that an elder's children must be believers in Christ. However, the language means that they are to be faithful to their parents by not being unruly. An elder is not responsible for his children's salvation, but he is responsible for their general behavior. This, of course, assumes that the elder has children. Paul was not requiring an elder to have children.

335 More literally, *holy.*

336 The word *spiritually* is poetic elaboration. Paul assumes the reader understands being clean in the spiritual sense.

337 The Greek text shows that the defiled and unbelieving refer to the same people. Therefore, the defiled by definition are those who have not trusted Christ. Only by trusting Christ can one become clean in God's sight.

338 Literally, *our Savior, God.*

339 The Greek text fits a rule showing that *the blessed hope* and *appearance in glory* refer to the same thing. Also, *God* and *Savior* fit this rule as well. Jesus Christ is our great God and Savior.

340 Poetic elaboration on the word *redeem*, referring to the purchase of a slave's freedom.

341 *Which we had deemed as worth* is more literally *which we ourselves did.*

342 The word *King* is literally *Christ.*

343 The last two lines in this stanza are implied from the next verse.

344 No verb is expressed in the Greek text. Therefore, this is not a wish but an exclamation of fact. See 2 Corinthians 13:14 and Galatians 1:3 notes.

345 This is not a wish but an exclamation of fact as the Greek text makes clear. See 2 Corinthians 13:14 and Galatians 1:3 notes.

346 Greek copies vary between *within us* and *within you.* Both have good early support. The earliest copy reads *within you.*

347 The last three lines reflect very difficult Greek phrasing that poses a challenge in translating. A word-for-word translation reads, *in order that I may not say to you that you owe me besides even yourself.* How is this a purpose for paying Onesimus's debt? Paul is saying that if Onesimus owes Philemon anything, he (Paul) will pay it. However, Paul does not want Philemon to think that he has to pay him back even though Philemon owes him his life. How does Philemon owe Paul his life? Paul most likely brought him to Christ. He completely releases Onesimus from feeling any financial obligation. He only wants his spiritual obligation.

348 *God's gift* is literally a verb meaning *freely give.* The Greek text reflects an unnamed subject as the giver giving Paul as a gift to Philemon. That unnamed subject is obviously God.

349 The word *your* is in the plural in the Greek. So Paul is not referring to just Philemon but to all believers whom he mentioned in the opening verses.

350 This last line is poetic elaboration. Paul is not giving a wish but an exclamation of fact as the Greek text makes clear. See 2 Corinthians 13:14 and Galatians 1:3 notes.

www.ingramcontent.com/pod-product-compliance
Lightning Source LLC
Chambersburg PA
CBHW021051080526
44587CB00010B/209